Bridge Work: Essays on Mythology, Literature and Psychology

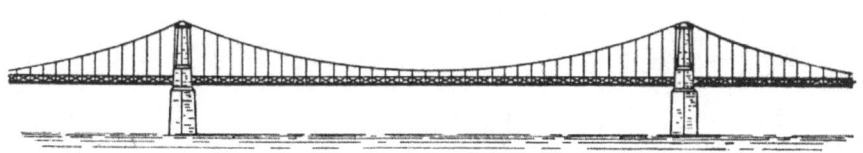

DENNIS PATRICK SLATTERY

Cover art: "Three Bridges" by Anita Luellen
(www.lightsideimages.com)
Cover design: Jennifer Leigh Selig (www.jenniferleighselig.com)

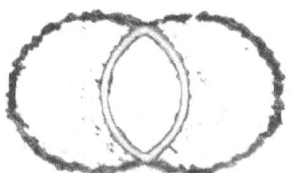

MANDORLA BOOKS
CARPINTERIA, CA
WWW.MANDORLABOOKS.COM

DEDICATION

To my family for their unwavering support:
Sandy, Matt, McKenzie, Steve, Francesca, Ellie, Marty, Bob,
Charlene, Bill, Mary Beth, Phil, Andrea, Chad, Kevin, Marian and
Kathy.

This [numerical] "field," which we take to represent the structural outlines of the collective unconscious, is organized around the central archetype of the Self.

~Marie-Louise von Franz
Number and Time: Studies in Jungian Thought 30

CONTENTS

Foreword   ix

Introduction   xiii

I
FORMAL ESSAYS

1 Complex Nature and Mimetic Desire: Towards a Bio-   1
   Mimesis of Psyche and Matter

2 Mythos, Logos and the Politics of Justice   11

3 Dante's *Terza Rima* in *The Divine Comedy*: The Road of   25
   Therapy

4 Mystic Faces, History's Traces: Joseph Campbell, Mystic   47

5 Violent Designs: Imagining Violence as Physical and   69
   Fictional

6 Boxing Piety's Shadow   83

7 Hestia: Goddess of the Heart(h)   93

8 Myth, Method and Mythopoiesis: James Hillman's   103
   Archetypal Psychology as Poetic Archeology

9 What is Myth and the God-Image?   111

10 Aesthetics, Politics, Ethics: An Emerging Trinity of   121
   Imagination in James Hillman's *City and Soul*

II
CULTURAL ESSAYS

11   The Terrible Cost of Trust   131

12   Science, Math—and Myth. Why Not?   135

13   Holy Terror: The White Whale and the American Mythos   139

14   Lucy Under Glass   145

15   The Confluence of Remembering and Forgetting   149

16   Called to a Cohearant Life   165

17   The Myth of Memorial Day   179

18   Growth: When a Myth No Longer Serves   183

19   Poetry as Frame and as Form   187

20   Myth and Wonder   193

     About the Author   199

     Acknowledgments   201

FOREWORD

I have had the pleasure of knowing Dennis Patrick Slattery now for fifteen years...

Forewords to books often start out this way, with the "foreworder" staking claim to the relationship which gives one the "authority" to forward anything. Foreword becomes a forward, like we forward an email or an article with a foreword such as "Thought of you when I read this," or "You'll find this interesting."

So who am I to foreword this book for you, to forward this book to you, beckoning you toward it like a literary pusher, whispering "Hey. You. I got something you're gonna wanna read"?

First and foremost, I am Dennis' student. He blew into my classroom in 1999 like a great nor'easter, nearly knocking me out of my comfortable seat and flooding my mind with his love of literature. I mean, I thought I loved literature until I met Dennis! I sat perfectly still in the eye of the storm, transfixed, as I watched him pace the room, novel in hand, gesticulating and articulating and pontificating and beatificating every word in every sentence in every paragraph of the *text de jour*. (The man could read a soup-stained diner menu into song!). Learning literature from Dennis was a singular experience of synesthesia. I would hear him read a sentence and suddenly I could smell the nouns and taste the verbs and feel the adjectives curled up in the palm of my hand.

Second and serendipitously, I am Dennis' colleague. We both teach at Pacifica Graduate Institute in Carpinteria, California, though in different departments and usually on different campuses. Still, I sometimes walk by his classroom and though I cannot hear his distinct words, the sonorous sound of his voice makes my mouth suddenly water, and I have to keep my knees from shifting direction and my body from billowing back into his classroom again. He taught me that time spent opening a class with a poem is time well spent, and he taught me to cock my head towards my students when they made comments, no matter how peculiar or outlandish, and reply, "Say more," as if they had everything to teach you (which they do) and you had better listen (which he did).

Third and quite thrillingly, I am Dennis' co-editor. I am still not sure why he approached me to co-edit a book of essays with him, which would become *Reimagining Education: Essays on Reviving the Soul of Learning*. It was the single most collegial gesture anyone had ever made toward me, an act of great generosity from a senior colleague to one far his junior. I enjoyed every moment of collaborating with him on the project, and I believe he did as well, for after we got our first baby safely into the world and tucked into the bookshelf, we created a second literary love-child together: *The Soul Does Not Specialize: Revaluing the Humanities and the Polyvalent Imagination*. There is a common theme to these books, of course, which is reviving and revaluing the imagination, a passion project for us both, and dare I say, that which has animated every corner of his career. This began in his childhood, when he stayed home (love)sick to read books by flashlight under the covers of his bed-turned-fort (a story he recounts in the latter volume).

I have longed to lie between the covers of another book with him, and he gave my longing flesh when he cast me into another role in his life. Fourth and for this text, I am Dennis' publisher. I designed and built the cover, I laid out every page, I read each word and edited so few. To do so was both an honor and a joy. Reading a collection of Dennis' essays is to find oneself constantly in a state of delight, even while agitated or dislocated or even perforated by his words. Each essay surprises; each essay moves; each essay sucker-punches you with an aha and an insight; each essay tickles you with a particularly facile turn of phrase.

That's only the content, the carefully crafted writing itself. What's more, however, is what each essay reveals about the writer himself. Each essay exposes a man fully engaged by life; each essay discloses the limitless leaping nature of his agile imagination. **He asks questions**: What do we remember and what do we forget, and why? (in Chapter 15, "The Confluence of Memory and Forgetting"). **He pays homage:** to archetypal psychologist James Hillman and his poetic imagination (in Chapter 8, "Myth, Method and Mythopoesis: James Hillman's Archetypal Psychology as Poetic Archeology"), to the goddess Hestia (in Chapter 7, "Hestia: Goddess of the Heart(h)"). **He disturbs our peace** (in Chapter 5, "Violent Designs: Imagining Violence as Physical and Fictional"). **He meditates on a single word**: piety (in Chapter 6, "Boxing Piety's Shadow"); trust (in Chapter 11, 'The Terrible Cost of Trust"). **He challenges and critiques:** growth and development are not always virtues (in Chapter 18, "Growth: When a Myth No Longer Serves"); America has a terribly paradoxical relationship to justice (in Chapter 2, "Mythos, Logos and the Politics of Justice"). **He riffs on rhymes** (in Chapter 3, "Dante's *Terza Rima* in *The Divine Comedy*: The Road of Therapy"). **He celebrates myth** (in Chapter 20, "Myth and Wonder"); **he celebrates poetry** (in Chapter 19, "Poetry as Frame and as Form"); **he celebrates hominids** (in Chapter 14, "Lucy Under Glass"). Hominids, for god's sake! Is there nothing beyond this man's reach?

Stated simply, using another metaphor, *the man's got moves*, and though his moves are on display in 23 books, I like to think they especially dance in this vivid and vivifying volume. And so I forward this book to you with these forewords, because fifth and forever, I am Dennis' fan.

Jennifer Leigh Selig, Ph.D.

Author of *Integration: The Psychology and Mythology of Martin Luther King, Jr. and His (Unfinished) Therapy With the Soul of America*

INTRODUCTION

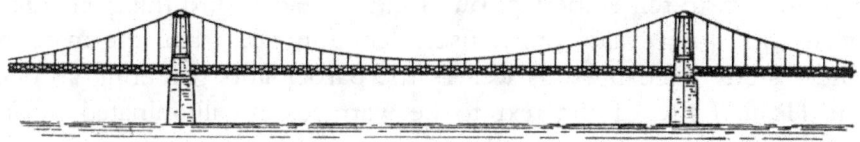

Alchemy is an old science, but also a new science that
is only now beginning to unfold. It reflects upon the
mystery of relations between things, and upon one's
relationship to the cosmos.
~Nathan Schwartz Salant, "Introduction"
to *Jung on Alchemy* 19

What is great in man is that he is a bridge,
and not a goal.
~Nietzsche, qtd. in Coleman Barks' "Introduction" to
Rumi: Bridge to the Soul 5

Whether it be the text of words or the text of the world, when
we enter either we are already constructing a field of relationships
between self and other. Lately I have been paying closer attention to
the creation of this field in the classroom as well as in my own
personal reading. I have discovered that it takes approximately 70-80
minutes, once the work for that class is presented and engaged, for
the force of the field to be felt. A landscape or terrain is created in
the triad that is present: we as readers, the text or the theme under
discussion, and that which arises from the two. In 45 years in the

classroom, as I reflect on the time I have spent in this sacred space, this pattern has been present; only now, at this moment in my teaching career, do I see the deep pattern of learning itself take shape as a universal principle of journeying from a state of not knowing to one of understanding. The level of this experience may vary, but not the pattern that governs it.

Reading into the field, or teaching into the field are both rituals of self-mythologizing as the work gains ground and takes hold and bites in. This field of energy and force is where deep learning occurs; it cannot happen with rote memorization or learning for the test. Those two dispositions end-stop field-making, and with it any learning worth remembering. But if in the field a third thing emerges, what C.G. Jung called the transcendent function, then the material under study is changed as well as the participants gathering around the Hestian fire of the text to be warmed and illuminated by its presence.

Many of you know the film of years past, *Field of Dreams* starring Kevin Costner. It is based on the magical and sweepingly entertaining novel, *Shoeless Joe* by W.P. Kinsella. Published in 1982 and treated so imaginatively by D. Stephenson Bond in his book, *Living Myth*, it tells the story of an ordinary Iowa farmer, Ray Kinsella, who is called by a radio announcer's voice to put the field in play. As Ray relaxes on his porch one evening in spring he hears the voice offer him one observation: "If you build it, he will come" (3). "He" is none other than a famous baseball player from the past, Shoeless Joe Jackson. If Ray builds the field, Shoeless Joe, as well as a host of other long-dead players will show up to play once more the game that defined each of their identities. Ray reflects on the announcer's directive: "A three hour lecture or a 500 page guide book could not have given me clearer direction.... That was all the instructions I ever received" (4). When, after putting the field in place, most of which labor he performed himself, and the games begin to be played on what could be called a *temenos*, a sacred space of the imagination, only certain spectators are granted the privilege of seeing it progress. For others, there is nothing to see, so they scratch their heads wondering what it is they are missing.

Heeding the call to adventure and following the form of the perennial baseball field—its bases, its measurements between bases, the size of the outfield—all open for Ray, his wife Anne, their daughter Karin and their collie Carmeletia Pope (4), a life both magical and mythical as history itself awakens from a long slumber in the figure of the players who now return regularly to reestablish the sport and construct a bridge between their historical past and Ray's promising present.

With some important similarities in place, the essays in this volume are my baseball fields; the players for whom they are built are any of you who venture into one or another of them to play with their ideas. The three bases of my field are composed of the following: first base: Mythology; second base: Literature; and third base: Psychology. Giving the rules some latitude, however, no one needs to run the bases in that order. Enter where you wish to play the game of exploring and scoring any new insights that work for you.

These fields are what I have been playing on and in for decades. I continue to explore my long-time interest in the deep relationships that exist between mythology, mytho-poetics and psychology. When possible, I enjoy mixing the three in the classroom, in talks to various groups I am invited to speak to, and in riting personal myth retreats to see what new connections can sprout from such relationships. I am as interested in considering the rhyme scheme of Dante's *Divine Comedy* as I am in why Memorial Day is such an important holiday for Americans to ritualize annually. I wonder as well about what it is that stokes violence either in the individual or in nations who continually attempt to dismantle one another over an idea or an ideology. I wonder about the marvel of being called to a work, as Ray Kinsella is as he sits on the veranda after a day of planting corn, seeding the earth to grow what will nourish others. But then something intervenes into his life that allows him to choose to cease all practical activity in order to build and carefully maintain a baseball field carved out amidst the corn stalks. His soul shifts in the process from farming to myth-making.

Bridge Work as Field Work

Creating interactive fields between disciplined ways of knowing and building bridges share a host of common properties. The quote of Nietzsche's above takes us to the title of this present volume: *Bridge Work: Essays on Mythology, Literature and Psychology*. Stepping or driving onto a bridge is akin to entering a field, one that consists of relations between this side and that far side to which one may be heading. The metaphor is an apt one for learning. To see by means of a multiplicity of disciplines is bridge work. Pausing and inhabiting a bridge for a short time is field work's space and place. A bridge is fundamentally connective tissue between two seemingly separate landscapes or territories. Building bridges is analogous to crafting relationships between contrasts, linking at the same instance differences to allow for recognizing how they may in fact be similar or share similar properties. A bridge expands one's range of understanding by what it joins; standing on a bridge allows one to see at least two realms at once with a simple turn of the head. As the head turns so may the pen. Bridges also carry a magical cache about them and in some instances convey a grandeur, as anyone knows who has crossed the Brooklyn Bridge, the Golden Gate Bridge or any other whose expanse in the air can take the breath away and whose vista can break open a narrow corridor of vision in order to gain a panoramic perch on the world.

Life below a bridge may also place one in a very different landscape. It can be a place of protection as well as a space of great vulnerability. How often, for instance, in riding motorcycles these past 45 years have I sought out and accelerated towards a road bridge to avoid the ferocity of approaching thunderstorms and winds that disallowed my journey to continue. There is then temporariness to inhabiting a bridge; one enters a bridge to cross over or to cross back and forth. At times one may linger or hover on a bridge for a keener sense of the landscape, but the time on bridges seems to be shorter than that spent on either side. Like a field, it is a temporary locale. The baseball game must eventually end.

I use these two very intimate figures, field and bridge, to intern how the essays in this volume are my bridges to understanding what they share, what they finally claim as either unique or different. In fact, where the two sides of the bridge or the respective fields of mythology, literature and psychology share differences may also in fact harbor similarities if we can see far or deeply enough to imagine them through the aperture of relationship.

I believe the soul's intrinsic nature is to build bridges and inhabit them, to relate, to connect, to be in kinship with others without suffocating difference. The bridge is one of the richest architectural archetypes to promote such relationships. In a manner of speaking, bridges connect fields; they allow for both independence as well as interdependence. In other words, bridges allow one to have it both ways. As they allow the chance to inhabit a suspended place, a place from which to hover for a time, bridges encourage wondering. Hovering temporarily—for its nature is to be brief—allows one to locate where things connect. Moving too quickly across a bridge cancels such gazing. We note what we see when we hover, then embellish it in recollection. Yet even in recollection we bridge something from the past with something more current.

We enter, then, a field of bridge work wherein something new has an on-going invitation to present itself so readers may wonder more about its possibilities. Wonder is at the heart of learning. The last chapter entertains the place and nature of wonder and, fittingly, it appears at the end. By adopting a disposition of wonder over mastery, something of the mystery of what is studied unfurls or blossoms in the field. Reading and writing, the actions that created this volume, are in a very real way both "field work" and "bridge work." Fields are terrains of value and insight. These essays explore the fertile fields of psyche, poiesis and mythos by integrating the sensibility indigenous to each. The consequence is, I believe, some new insights about their relationships. What these three forms of expression share is a "poetic basis of mind" that James Hillman insists "is the selective logic operating in the plots of our lives," by which he means the logic of mythos, mythology (*Healing Fiction* 12). Such a unique purview that governed his own unique form of exploring from a multitude of bridges, is shared by all three of the areas included in the present volume. All share as well a common overriding pattern, the pattern of mimesis, or imitation of some deep action of the soul that the works under investigation/imagination mirror. By this term mimesis I mean a making, in language, an analogy of an experience that mythologizes events of our lives into creative insights that form our personal myth. Analogies are among the most rich and elegant forms of bridge work.

My hope is that the essays contribute to the impulse of psyche to create story, to narrate itself into the world. Such narratives are not arrested at the level of poiesis but continue on and down, from psychology to ontology, on a path that transcends any individual story, yet includes it in the telling. An interpenetration of the works' structures with our own composition as readers is as integral to the act of interpretation as any theory that may guide one's reading.

Interpretation is at once an interpenetration wherein psyche and poetry are both engaged in a mutual act of making and shaping as well as discovering a unique coherent form to inform one's understanding at the deepest layers of imagination. Both involve a deepening of *gnosis*, which is a form of underworld knowing essential to the deepening bridge work that depth psychology insists on and promotes. Both experiences, in addition, are consciously embodied and ask that we remember our own incarnational reality in the process of the narrative. My efforts will be justified if readers are compelled to build their own bridges from the masonry included here so both fields and bridges may extend their life expectancy and encourage the construction of further bridges and fields.

Works Cited

Barks, Coleman. *Rumi: Bridge to the Soul: Journeys into the Music and Silence of the Heart.* Trans. Coleman Barks, A.J. Arberry and Nevit Ergin. New York: HarperCollins, 2007.

Hillman, James. *Healing Fiction.* Woodstock, Conn: Spring Publications, 1983.

Kinsella, W.P. *Shoeless Joe.* Boston: Houghton-Mifflin, 1999.

Schwartz-Salant, Nathan. "Introduction." *Jung on Alchemy.* Selected and Introduced by Nathan Schwartz-Salant. Princeton: Princeton UP, 1995. 1-43.

I
FORMAL ESSAYS

CHAPTER 1

COMPLEX NATURE AND MIMETIC DESIRE: TOWARDS A BIO-MIMESIS OF PSYCHE AND MATTER

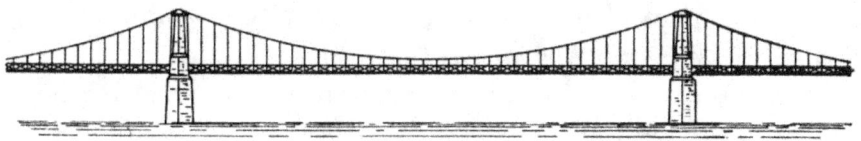

O Nature, and O soul of man! How far beyond all
utterance are your linked analogies! Not the smallest
atom stirs or lives in matter, but has its
cunning duplicate in mind.
~Captain Ahab in *Moby-Dick* 264

I begin this presentation[1] daunted before I finish the first sentence. Dr. Lori Pye's vision and her task set before us all is enormous, even magnificent, in its difficulty. But I remember her from one course specifically: Epic Imagination. So it makes sense to me: her imagination is indeed epic; in fact, no other poetic genre will characterize her in what she insists that each of us does in this rich and varied conference, namely: no less than prescribe what a shift in consciousness would include as we tease the sciences and the humanities towards conversation with one another again, as they did, for example, for centuries, and before the advent of a philosophy of materialism that, beginning innocently enough, gradually shouldered

1

out of the way any other paradigm for perceiving the created order. My best standard to suggest a time when the dialogue between the sciences and the humanities, indeed between all seven facets of the gem of the liberal arts, is Dante Alighieri's *Commedia*, written in the 14th century.

In his age, the Trivium, consisting of grammar, rhetoric and dialectic, held court and partied regularly with, the Quadrivium: music, arithmetic, astronomy and geometry. In the Middle Ages in Western Europe there were indeed seven ways of looking at a blackbird such that the act of learning was multi-souled and poly-valent. What this present conference prescribes as its internal *apologia* is a retrieval, a recycling and a renewal in a true ecological dynamics, of what we once had, like the earthly paradise itself, we lost and now must, of necessity, re-member back into the communal and individual psyche. The Anglican priest Bede Griffiths, who left England to live in an ashram in India to meditate and write, is one of our most profound thinkers of the dilemma, which he outlines with great economy and insight in his book, *A New Vision of Reality: Western Science, Eastern Mysticism and Christian Faith*.

Early on he diagnoses the malady of materialism which galloped with great force through any historical resistances posted to forestall it, from a method of science to a philosophy of being, from a way of perceiving matter to a definition of it, and from **a** way of perception to **the** way. Materialism is indeed, as Griffiths explores it, an interpretation (9). The good news, however, is that through biology, physics as well as the writings of C.G. Jung, James Hillman, Marie-Louise von Franz and others, that earlier sense of form that Aristotle believed was both real and operative in matter, is being retrieved in the work of physicist Fritjof Capra, Cambridge biologist Rupert Sheldrake, physicist and philosopher David Bohm, physicist F. David Peat, biologist of complexity theory Brian Goodwin and others, wherein formative principles, energic forces are also at work in the implicate order of being, that matter itself is continually being in-formed by fields, forces and perhaps even fate, as Michael Conforti's own work as well as his Assisi Institute confirm annually in a conference in Italy that studies patterns in psyche and matter that sustain all parts together in "linked analogies." Such linkage is acquiring new language in the work of biologist Dean Radin, whose new work, *Entangled Minds*, proceeds along similar grooves. He asserts that physicists suspect "that entanglement extends to everything in the universe, because as far as we know, all energy and matter emerged from a single primordial Big Bang" ("The Physics of Our Entanglement" 58).

It is indeed a big story, as epic as is this conference's theme and interest by you participants and presenters. So let us use this conference to create a story as big as the white whale, which, you recall in that marvelous tale, is big enough, grand enough, ubiquitous enough and mystical enough, to create an analogue of leviathan, as Ishmael suggests: "after sounding to a great depth, he transports himself with such vast swiftness to the most widely distant points . . . he creates a world of rumors" (158). Let us, in whale fashion, create a world of rumors by means of our narrative. And let our "unsullied jet" squirt gallons of ink across the globe with new writings of a tenderer heart's determined desire. In doing so, we may get an edge on the status quo of thought.

I wish now to move this presentation to the 19th century to retrieve a sonnet by one of the most poignant Romantic poets of nature, William Wordsworth. He, along with Samuel Coleridge, John Keats and other Romantic poets, knew the cost of losing psyche in nature and the natural proclivities of soul to be in relation to the landscape that promotes vegetation. Think of how far we have moved from the vegetative soul in the phrase, "veg out," which means essentially, to do nothing. Here is Wordsworth's sonnet, one of the most famous in his poetic reservoir, which reasons will quickly become apparent:

The World is Too Much with Us

The world is too much with us, late and soon,
Getting and spending, we lay waste our powers;
Little we see in Nature that is ours;
We have given our hearts away, a sordid boon!
This Sea that bares her bosom to the moon;
The winds that will be howling at all hours,
And are up-gathered now like sleeping flowers;
For this, for everything, we are out of tune;
It moves us not.—Great God! I'd rather be
A Pagan suckled in a creed outworn;

So might I, standing on this pleasant lea,
Have glimpses that would make me less forlorn;
Have sight of Proteus rising from the sea;
Or hear old Triton blow his wreathed horn. (Meyer 766)

I have learned it "by heart," a wonderful phrase, because I wanted it portable, to say it repeatedly, to let it open up, to gift me with a poetic angle into the arena we are all working, each in his/her own way, according to the mythos that moves us. Moreover, if we do not include the heart-knowledge of the earth, to feel the earth in a heart-felt way, then there will be no conversation leading to change in consciousness. Knowing "by-heart" gives us back ourselves, in the sonnet mirror of our own devising. I wish to spend a bit more time in the 19th century in just a moment, for their voices sounded the alarm in capital letters of the divorce from the natural order that began centuries before.

But these romantic spirits put a head and a heart on the crisis. In a similar way that the denial of global warming, now finally dissolving today, like a sweating iceberg in Antarctica, we were slow to hear Wordsworth's lament over the loss of the mythic spirits in matter, and for some reason then, matter, in its own ironic way, ceased to matter. The soul that animated matter was discarded and with it, a language to describe the earth.

But let's allow a physicist to speak, one of my favorites, David Bohm, whose small, beautifully crafted book, *On Creativity*, will repay tenfold any time you surrender to it. Its force resides in how it reads like a lyric poem to the creative process that is inclusive in its grand orbit. Two observations he makes, one early on, one halfway through his musings, begin to answer the "How" part of this talk as well as this conference.

As he creates a dialogue between artist and scientist, he observes that "what the scientist can learn from art is first of all to appreciate the artistic spirit in which beauty and ugliness are, in effect, taken as sensitive emotional indicators of truth and falsity" (37). Not accepting this disclosure, the scientist and artist will continue to foreclose on one another's knowledge and wisdom bases as irrelevant to their own discoveries. Then Bohm turns the question around: "what can the artist learn from science?" Again, he invites the language of appreciation: the artist "could appreciate the scientific

4

spirit of an unbiased objective approach to structure, which demands that it be internally coherent and coherent with relevant facts, *whether one likes it or not*" (37, original emphasis). And then the closing on both perspectives: he claims that as "scientific truth is found to be inseparable from artistic beauty, so artistic beauty may be seen to be inseparable from truth in the scientific sense" (37), especially if science is allowed a greater orbit of meaning than is generally vouchsafed. Two words in his description arrest my eye: appreciation and beauty.

These two qualities of soul offer more possible ways of imagining the conversation that Lori calls us to cultivate. Such qualities send up a signal flare of caution here: I am beginning to be suspicious of the language couching the environmental crisis, terms like the one I just used. Others include: *global warming, inconvenient truth, rising earth's temperature, global crisis, melting icecaps*—you get the idea. We must beware of being trapped into a lexicon that then determines the orbit of the conversation; sociology replaces a more imaginal inquiry and material urgency forestalls once again diving deep to the center of the crisis, which is not material but spiritual. We must be vigilant of the populist language that clichés us into seeing along a narrow corridor. Indeed, Al Gore is Pan in the complex, piping hot facts at us all, with the best of intentions.

But does all the above miss the imagination of the earth, and more, the imagination of culture's voice in the vortex of reconciliation? If a conversation is going to ensue, then all parties must holster all clichés, standard responses, knee-jerk conventional, safe reactions, for nothing less than the survival of language itself is in the mix. The bigger question for me is to reimagine the *What,* not the *How*, of the content and the soul that animates these phenomena, both natural and cultural. Like a seat or a room or a restaurant promising to be "smoke-free," we must have a conversation with signs marking a "jargon-free" zone of inquiry.

Bohm has just laid out as foundation one facet of *mimesis*, a word that Aristotle popularized in his *Poetics* in the 5th century BCE to mean a making or a shaping into a coherent form, from what I would ascribe to *prima materia,* what had not before existed. If, therefore, the imagination driving the engines of science and those driving the motors of art were to open to one another in fearless courage, each would discern that its respective disciplines indeed are mimetic of one another and could fruitfully benefit from accepting that each shapes and forms the patterns discovered in the other. All is indeed inter-dependent, a sharp arrow that cuts into the flesh of autonomy as the West's prevailing ethos.

In addition, about half way through his discussion of the creative soul, Bohm introduces a section entitled: "On art, science, mathematics, and their general significance for 'the good'" (80). If, as he insists in this section, that the etymology of the word "art" is "to fit," and that it forms the foundation of words like *articulate, artifice, artisan, a builder*, then the word has more fitting meanings than simply an anemic one that engages aesthetics exclusively. The word *science,* by contrast, means *to know*. Therefore, art offers fitting knowing in its own scientific way. Might we extrapolate from this moment of insight and conjecture that the natural world, in its own artistry and ways of knowing, are mimetic of human nature's knowing and aesthetic sense? Is this one of many interstices where conversation can begin, in this gap of not-knowing? It is what I believe and propose. Let psyche and science converge in the gap, where neither knows with their usual certainty, where the boots slip on the sides of the moist hill and where hiking poles are a necessity for support.

Now a brief excursion towards C.G. Jung's "On Psychic Energy" by way of another 19th century voice, Ralph Waldo Emerson, and more specifically, to his powerful essay, "Nature." In it Emerson also engages deeply the idea of bio-mimesis that Jung develops further in his insights on energy. When Emerson wrote, he carried the spirited conviction that nature still carried the story of human being in its wheat fields, its rivers and blossoms, as well as in its storms, its violence and in its destructive interludes. The world as mirror rather than the world as product was the controlling metaphor that shaped a world view.

His musings retrieve the sensate natural order experienced by ancient peoples wherein "the fall of snowflakes in still air," or "blowing of sleet over a wide sheet of water and over plains waving rye fields" comprise the "music and religion of the most ancient religion" (216). If what human beings create as architecture, as towns, as edifices of civilization do not carry with them the original beauty of the natural order, the ministries of ugliness will be their greatest achievement. Magnificence in cultural inventions, he promises, is only achieved by reflecting the magnificence in nature. Her domain is embodied, psychic and spiritual. In fact, his claim is that "Nature is loved by what is best in us. It is loved as the city of God . . . " (218). Now in each of his illustrations lurks the analogic or mimetic psyche, one which mirrors and has mirrored to itself the world of matter. Bio-mimesis must then be extended beyond bios alone to include the physical world in all its artificial naturalness as well as her deep energies that offer sustenance, repetition and continuity.

And yet, he is not content with simply imitating or miming the flow of energy in the natural order, for there is something in us as mortals that transcends nature as well. When Emerson watches a brook's stream in front of him, he muses: "if our own life flowed with the right energy, we should shame the brook" (219). A paradox therefore arises in his grasp of Nature and human nature; as Nature keeps to her own laws in the deepest aesthetic panoplies of beauty, so is what is claimed to be "artificial" also natural; he closes the dichotomy that has grown up like lichen on the backside of this split. His example here is both comic and profound: "The smoothest curled courtier in the boudoirs of a palace has an animal nature, rude and aboriginal as a white bear, omnipotent to its own ends, and is directly related . . . to Himmaleh mountain chains and the axis of the globe" (220).

Nature, he goes on to delineate in quick succession, is profligate, excessive, a bit of a bigot and a lunatic, full of exaggeration, a bit mocking, able to lead us on to nowhere, often keeps no faith with us, approximates often over being precise, is deceitful, appears to mortals as existing elsewhere, not in front of us, often defers in time rather than satisfies in the immediate present, promotes an absence, not often a presence and a satisfaction, and finally is most often mysterious and full of secrets. Then, towards the end, he confesses where he has been heading: "Nature is the incarnation of a thought, and turns to thought again, as ice becomes water and gas. The world is mind precipitated and the volatile essence is forever escaping again into the state of free thought" (226). I suggest right here that Emerson is intimating an energy flow of knowledge between psyche and matter, between mind and nature, between nature and culture. Ahab's observation at the beginning of this excursus is a first cousin to Emerson's insight.

So what indeed is the idea of nature, and its connection with our own psychic and spiritual being embodied? Even more critical: how might science and psyche convene over a rereading and reconsideration of less the content than the model of Johannes Kepler (1571-1630) that Jung and his engaging physicist colleague, Wolfgang Pauli, collaborated in studying. Out of this model for today's split disciplines came the publication *The Interpretation of Nature and Psyche* wherein Jung contributed a long chapter on synchronicity and Pauli a chapter entitled "The Influence of Archetypal Ideas on the Scientific Theories of Kepler."

As both a mystic and a scientist, Kepler revealed through his writing as much a worldview as it was the content of his physics. This kind of cross-referenced *zeitgeist* is what we need today to further energize the conversation, and not just between science and psyche, but as well with the mystical imagination. This last should not be left out at any cost. Huston Smith is one of the most popular voices crying in the desert to find a place of reconciliation between science and religion. His arguments ought to be as much a part of the roundtable discussion as any others' works.

Pauli nailed it when he wrote, in an unpublished essay, "Modern Examples of Background Physics," where he recounts that in the 17th century physics of Kepler, the physical and symbolic participated together as a unity, leading both men to intuit the connective tissue between their disciplines through Kepler's work. By means of these "instincts of the imagination," Pauli and Jung, I wrote in an extended review of their correspondence, "launched an intense exchange to discover correspondences—a network of analogies that would excite and convince both men of the analogies that hold *psyche* and *physis* together in an intimate, powerful and invisible partnership" (Slattery 4). In such a mutual feeding off of one another's brilliance, *with an openness to be changed and to change*, Pauli helped Jung become an atomic physicist and Jung Pauli a depth psychologist. Jung was later to write in "The Structure and Dynamics of the Self," one of his key statements on this relationship: "Psyche cannot be totally different from matter, for how otherwise could it move matter? And matter cannot be alien to psyche, for how else could matter produce psyche? Psyche and matter exist in one and the same world, and each partakes of the other..." (*Collected Works* 9,2 ¶413).

What is important about this friendship of mutual respect from two leaders in their fields is that it can serve as a paradigm, a model for manners in a discussion where each voice is less concerned with staking claims and more with musing on matter, less obsessed with preserving their status and the status quo of their knowledge, more open and generous to the other's attitude towards what and how they know. That's one.

The other is more southern California, and I say it with deep oceanic affection. What undergirds any success with conversation that can be carried into action is a renewed love of the earth. My sense is that many have fallen out of love of the earth for herself, not to develop, change, escape to, pander, manage, exploit or prod for more production. Eros and earth have parted ways. I think we need to love the earth before we can know the earth in a new and intimate way. Love is a way of imagining particulars, as a way of paying attention, being attentive. Loving, Dante instructed us so beautifully, is indeed a way of knowing; if we love the earth in due measure, not excessively or minimally or distortedly, then our knowing of her carries the capacity to lead immediately to behaviors that don't simply cease abusing her, but in fact set in place conditions by which she can recover and flourish and share again the bounty of her perennial largesse.

Finally, I am inspired by something that Thomas Moore writes in an exquisite "Introduction" to the monk Thomas Merton's book of observations on spirit, politics and nature, *Conjectures of a Guilty Bystander*. From his Merton studies Moore concludes that "the neglect of the earth is a religious problem," an angle that is "often missing in current debates about the environment, which remain within a secular framework" (x). This narrower corridor of debate limits what can be transformed in attitude, temperament and spirit if a shift in emotional inflection towards the earth is to be realized on a national and global field, in the same way that the elimination of trans fats, now even performed on Girl Scout cookies, has become a national religious exercise. To lose, or not even allow in to the conversation of the earth's fate—the new nomenclature for the crisis—the religious sensibility, denudes the forest of this conversation.

Someday, it is my hope, that the mystic as monk and lay person, the educator, the politician, the poet and the populace will engage the same quantum space in service to earth's resurrection. Now THAT would be the place for us to gather again to effect a sea change in consciousness that would include such a panoply of participants. Such is my final hope.

Endnote

[1] The conference was "Nature and Human Nature: Changing Perspectives" sponsored by the Foundation for Mythological Studies, Ojai, California, March 16-18, 2007.

Works Cited

Bohm, David. *On Creativity*. Ed. Lee Nichol. London: Routledge, 1998.

Emerson, Ralph Waldo. "Nature." *The Essays of Ralph Waldo Emerson: The First and Second Series*. New York: The Heritage P, 1934. 214-26.

Griffiths, Bede. *A New Vision of Reality: Western Science, Eastern Mysticism and Christian Faith*. Springfield, Illinois. Templegate Publishers, 1990.

Jung, C. G. *The Collected Works of C.G. Jung*. Trans. R.F.C. Hull. Vol. 9_2. Princeton: Princeton UP, 1967.

Jung, C.G. and Wolfgang Pauli. *The Interpretation of Nature and Psyche*. Bollingen Series LI. New York: Pantheon Books, 1958.

Melville, Herman. *Moby-Dick, or The Whale*. Ed. Harrison Hayford and Hershel Parker. Norton: New York, 1967. 1-470.

Moore, Thomas. "Introduction." Thomas Merton's *Conjectures of a Guilty Bystander*. New York: Image Books, 1989. x-xv.

Radin, Dean. "The Physics of Our Entanglements." *Spirituality and Health: The Soul/Body Connection*. Nov./Dec 2006. 56-59.

Slattery, Dennis Patrick. *Atom and Archetype: the Pauli/Jung Letters. The San Francisco Jung Institute Library Journal*. Vol. 22, No.1, 2003. 5-11.

Wordsworth, William. "The World is Too Much With Us." *The Bedford Introduction to Literature*. 4th edition. Ed. Michael Meyer. Boston: Bedford Books of St. Martin's, 1996. 766.

CHAPTER 2

MYTHOS, LOGOS AND THE POLITICS OF JUSTICE

For men are easily spoilt; not everyone can bear
prosperity…. Especially should the laws provide
against anyone having too much power derived from
friends or from money; if he has, he and his followers
should be sent out of the country.
~Aristotle, *Politics*, n.d. Book V, chapter 8. 361

Shadowy Soft Spots

The immediate danger confronting one who wishes to reflect on
the political landscape of American governance and its relation or
lack thereof, to social justice, is to begin by entertaining them in too
literal a manner. Rather than a rush to literalize the terms, one might
pause long enough to pose an earlier question: what is the mythology
that drives the engines of American politics? The same might be
asked of social justice. For behind both impulses are theories, and
imbedded in theories are mythologies, which I understand as

governing patterns of values, even energy fields of understanding, that rest invisibly as force fields that influence and shape the perceptions of what is visible. Not tapping this deeper sensibility leaves us susceptible to the virus of literalism which freezes these organic entities into rigid mind sets, stiff opinions, or even self-righteous beliefs that resemble a form of *rigor mortis*. Our politics are our theories and our theories express underlying mythologies that govern them, often unconsciously. In fact, the less one accepts the reality of the individual and world psyche, the more powerful are the forces of theory as myth. Their intrinsic and innate power resides in their abilities to undo us in our conceptual impulses, even as we slumber during the process.

Moreover, our sense of social justice rests often on invisible edifices of epistemology. To express it another way, our ways of knowing—the *episteme* that directs them—is deeply connected to the mythos that gives them form and structure. Joseph Campbell, perhaps more than any other writer of the modern era, introduced mythology back into the cultural imagination as a respectable mode of inquiry. In an early section of *Thou Art That* entitled "What Myths Do," he claims multiple functions of any people's mythology. They are worth noting here at the outset:

> The first function of mythology is to arouse in the mind a sense of awe . . . through one of three ways of participating in it: by moving out, moving in, or effecting a correction. . . . The second function of a traditional mythology is interpretive, to present a consistent image of the order of the cosmos. . . . The third function of a traditional mythology is to validate and support a specific moral order, that order of the society out of which that mythology arose. . . . The fourth function of a traditional mythology is to carry the individual through the various stages and crises of life—that is, to help persons grasp the unfolding of life with integrity. (3-5)

If in this complex discussion of politics and justice the mythos is not addressed on a thoughtful and receptive level, rather than only on the rancorous level of logos, then expressing that relationship will be always half-baked, but perhaps with yeasty inflation, as it emerges prematurely out of the social oven.

Even earlier questions that I am compelled to pose are these: What is a just society? What does it look like? What are its governing images, its self-correcting myths as well as its shadowy underbelly? And even earlier: Is there an impulse in the soul that hungers for justice and virtue? Who is allowed to participate in such a world with a voice that will be heard? There is no way around it; politics and justice are psychological tendencies in the soul, even mythological dispositions, because they carry into the minds of individuals and the collective large fantasies of right and wrong. Further, what are the shadows that American politics and even tendencies to social justice transport? For if we ignore the shadowy images that are just below the surface of both politics and justice, we run the risk of exchanging one set of fantasies for another, one blueprint for change for another such that both end by leaving us right where we are. I mention at the close of this paragraph that I have consciously avoided the more traditional "How" and "Why" questions: "How" because then I am thrown into technique; "Why" because I am then caught in cause-effect relations that foreclose on exploring these gnarly and knotty dimensions of the common good.

The poet, playwright and political leader of the Czech Republic, Vaclav Havel, has written elegantly of the world's drama. His poetic sense is aided, not deflected, from his power as a humane leader. In December, 1955, at the site of Hiroshima during an international conference on hope, he addressed the audience with this insight:

> The only thing that can explain the existence of genuine hope is humanity's profound and essentially archetypal certainty— though denied or unrecognized a hundred times over—that our life on this earth is not just a random event . . . but that it is an integral component or link, however miniscule, in the great and mysterious order of Being, an order in which everything has a place of its own . . . and given its proper and permanent value. (239)

Our theories and our policies, as Havel's insights inform us, are surface ripples of a deeper mythology that shapes and forms them. Yet the mythos of politics or the psychic fields created by them churn under the floorboards but are not often given ample voice. So let's ask the question another way: What is the imagination of

American Politics? What images in the collective psyche propel impulses towards social justice? Both are acts of imagination, not just reasoned tracks of thought and action. I admit that I have certainly not read all of *The 9/11 Commission Report: Authorized Edition.* But one conclusion reached by those who composed it struck me regarding the present topic. Chapter 11, "Foresight—And Hindsight," included these words: "We believe the 9/11 attacks revealed four kinds of failures: in imagination, policy, capabilities, and management" (339). This discovery must be taken seriously; it is one of the startling admissions in the *Report* as far as I have read because it lifts the discussion out of simply and narrowly discursive reason as well as the anemic language that attends it, and places it instead in the realm of psyche and imagination. Is there an implication here that perhaps not just American politics but social justice as well must be reimagined and then languaged differently?

Animating a Cliché

When I hear the term "social justice" I think of fair wages, clean water, one's ability to advance in his/her work, muted control by authority over one's everyday life, the right to worship as one believes, a general sense of fair play in the spirit of a golden mean, a specter of freedom in thought, speech and actions, and a fair or at least adequate distribution of wealth. But these are the trappings of the visible realm that can easily occlude or disbar from conversation the soul of things, the animating principles that, while invisible, are no less tangible realities if our epistemology is courageous enough to expand to embrace them. So what about a conversation that includes the mythos of the polis or its epistemology—what are its tenets and tenants of knowing—that guide a political party, regime, candidate, or nation? Let it also include the connection between politics and Eros: Where is the juice and what is its flow through a political debate? Where does the adequacy of a political regime or the sense of social justice draw its lines of limitations? Is either caught in an obsessive mode of thought that forbids it to spread out beyond its own narcissism or narrowly defined causative sense of itself?

I bring this language in here to challenge a dangerous tendency in current American debates: So much of the language is impoverished, especially in its tendency to make individual lives and their vicissitudes into "Issues," a word that has come to flatten out the realities of persons' lives into abstractions by objectifying and thereby distancing self from any significant conversation that could actually change something. With "Issues" everything is modified to this sterile noun; all is made adjectival and thus subordinate to the soft, even gooey word: "Issues." If the discussion is to retrieve any imaginal energy, we must pay closer attention to the language used in the debates.

I believe language, vocabulary, metaphor, symbol, currently used in debates are anemic, bereft, narrow, shrunken, shriveled, and finally inadequate for today's complexities, just as the sound-bite is patently pathetic in trying to deploy nuance or subtlety. That, however, is a topic for another volume: Social Justice and Language. Consider the language of today's campaigns: *national safety, security, resolute, stay the course, get the job done, the American people want..., change, new direction, cut-and-run, no yielding, courage, bravery, simply rhetoric, new dawn, move forward, failure is not an option.* The language of obfuscation, while having the 10 second force of a sound-bite, actually inhibits, to my mind, any penetration of the particulars of reality that this vocabulary ostensibly refers to and conjures up in the mind. Quite the opposite: this vocabulary works to increase the kind of "psychic numbing" that the social critic Robert J. Lifton has characterized as the bane of the American mind when daily assaulted with news of violence, warfare and misfortune.

One more before shifting to American mythology. Missing far too often in the current discussions is not just imagination, which could allow for a poetics of debate, but a philosophic discourse as well. The prevailing fantasy is that one must follow the lead of the media's structure, which then becomes the dominant frame for the debate. This is a dangerous reversal of how public discussion should work. I therefore sense a desperate capitulation to the status of a national Attention Deficit Disorder driving the current debate of a faulty democracy. Not a good place to be. It is just a hair's breath away from Tyranny. I could launch right here into the ways studying the Humanities might make for a more discerning citizenry, but will refrain.

Let's add as well another category: Politics and the Sacred. The language of "separation of church and state" has been torqued grotesquely into a weapon by several factions, with devastating results. Not church but the sacred quality of citizenship would muster another range of topics. We might also return to beginnings of the political idea that animates the Western psyche instead of simply choosing to limp along with the same crippled rhetoric, the same sclerotic prose and the worn out, desperate clichés mentioned above, that attempt to substitute for thoughtful exchange. Therefore, to the terms of the current debate I wish to sign a form on the clipboard of the exhausted patient: "Do Not Resuscitate." Let the patient die, mercifully, etherized on the table. The patient is exhausted language, clichés, catch phrases and slogans; the language in the discussion on both sides appears pooped and in need of a complete death or a massive transfusion of new blood and words to enliven, even quicken the discourse. Perhaps nothing short of a new heart will do. I have this image of someone who, in the aftermath of a hurricane, where the house has been torn apart, desperately hammers a few new shingles on the rubbled roof, hoping to shore up its ruined grandeur.

Let me turn now to one of the prevailing myths that, while a bit tarnished and showing signs of fatigue, nonetheless governs huge swaths of the American psyche today.

America's Sustaining Mythos

One myth that governs this relationship has been expressed by many writers, one of whom most notably is the Cistercian monk and political activist Thomas Merton. Early in *Conjectures of a Guilty Bystander* he locates the central myth of America as a reformatting of "the earthly paradise." As a new land, it suffers no memory, no history, no residue or taint of the past: "The New-Found-Land was a world without *history,* therefore without sin, therefore a paradise" (34). It was thus a land that promised the suffering of Europe a fresh start in a wilderness of milk and honey "with one's hand in the hand of God..." (34).

With no deep memory to guide it, and with its temptation to erase the tribal memories of the new land, a version of the serpent in the primordial Garden (35), America's compass was already quivering in shaky air. True North was an idea rather than a concrete direction. The image or myth of the frontier continued her journey of innocence. Repeated successes further ingrained such a stance and disposition. Merton's reading is that success covered a multitude of sins and essentially allowed injustices to be leveled on America's own people and on others "outside the myth" such that the politics of America split and scurried from a full sense of justice for all.

Not until the Civil War did America fall into original sin, when the nation divided violently over whether a people exported and exploited by capitalism were to be free or enslaved as part of the machinery of prosperity. I would call the Civil War the great mythic divide between innocence and guilt, a chasm between politics and justice; we have not fully recovered from that deep national wound, which seems to be perpetuated in subsequent conflicts we find ourselves in, often wrapped in a faulty and threadbare security blanket of a too-literal idea of freedom. Here we can learn something about the nature of a mythology. The myth that a people chooses for itself as guide, or a myth that is foisted on them, directs their values, their beliefs, their prejudices, what they choose to remember and, perhaps more critically, what they choose, or prefer, to forget. A myth is deeply imbedded in our assumptions. It also sets the perimeters of the conversation and frames the debate in a too narrow lexicon. In my own thought, what separates American politics from the arena of social justice rests primarily on what we as a nation choose to remember and what we struggle to leave at the next rest stop, to keep at bay, to stiff-arm long enough until it yields and eventually vanishes completely.

Recollecting the Origin of an Idea

So let us remember and then recover for a moment some ideas about justice that defined the early contours of the Western mythos into which America enters as a late participant. The early Western philosophers Plato and Aristotle wrote extensively about the nature of justice, virtue, falsehood, leadership and the quality of life possible in the polis. For both of them, perhaps for different reasons, these qualities were bedrock for a democratic state to flourish.

In Book I of the *Republic*, Socrates is enjoying a conversation with a Greek citizen, Thrasymachus on the connection between justice and wisdom, and the sad consequences when they part company.

> Socrates: "For factions, Thrasymachus, are the outcome of injustice and hatreds and internecine conflicts, but justice brings oneness of mind and love. Is it not so?"

Thrasymachus readily assents, as Socrates continues:

> "If it is the business of injustice to engender hatred wherever it is found, will it not, when it springs up either among free men or slaves, cause them to hate and be at strife with one another, and make them incapable of effective action in common?"

To which his partner replies: "By all means."
   Socrates then pushes the force of injustice one step further:

> "And is it not apparent that its force is such that wherever it is found in city, family, camp, or in anything else, it first renders the thing incapable of co-operation with itself owing to faction and difference…?" (602)

Socrates reveals in this ancient text the marriage between politics and justice and their destructive tendencies when injustice rules the individual, the family or the city.
   Later, in the *Laws,* he uses the metaphor of "a polity," which "is like a ship or a living organism" (1491) and its health rests on the justice inherent in the character of its leaders:

> "For if the censors who are to approve our magistrates are better men themselves, and do their work with flawless and irreproachable justice, then there will be prosperity and true happiness for the whole of the nation and society, but if aught is amiss with the auditing of our magistrates, then the bonds of right which hold all branches of our social fabric together in one will be loosened…." (1491)

I return a last time to the *Republic* for a final insight by Socrates in his deepening discussion with Thrasymachus, wherein the former addresses the soul's work:

> "The soul, has it a work which you could accomplish with anything else in the world, as for example, management, rule, deliberation, and the like? Is there anything else than soul to which you could rightly assign these and say that they were its peculiar work?" to which his agreeable partner responds: "Nothing else." (604)

Socrates then questions the soul's relation to virtue: "Will the soul ever accomplish its own work well if deprived of its own virtue, or is this impossible? . . . And did we not agree that the excellence or virtue of soul is justice and defect injustice?" (604). The point of his strategy is to reveal that no matter how one slices the nature of justice, the just soul is happy, lives well, is virtuous and participates in excellence (604). My reading of these passages suggests that politics and social justice have no "and" between them; they are one and the same force in the polis and in the soul of the citizen.

Would that these memories of Socrates' discussions could find their way into the halls of Washington and to the state capitals to renew and revision the inextinguishable power of leadership and citizenship in a democracy.

Following Plato, yet pushing the discussion further, Aristotle reveals, first in Book IV of the *Politics*, the cherished place of a democracy in promoting justice, social or otherwise: "Therefore we should rather say that democracy is a form of government in which the free are rulers, and oligarchy one in which the rich rule. It is only an accident that the free are the many and the rich are the few"(325).

A few pages later, he elaborates the various faces a democracy may assume: "Of the forms of democracy, first comes that which is said to be based strictly on equality. In such a democracy, the law calls it justice that the poor should have no more power than the rich, and that neither should be masters, but both equal. For if liberty and equality, as is thought by some, are the chief characteristics of democracy, they will be best attained when all persons alike share in the government to the utmost" (328).

The danger of forms of oligarchy, by contrast, are that they exclude the poor: "the property qualification for any office is so high that the poor, although they form the majority, have no share in government. While it does not necessarily follow, there is a tendency of an oligarchy to furnish fertile breeding ground for a tyrant to attain absolute power" (328). In Book V of the *Laws*, Aristotle sums up the behavior of a tyrant: (1) the humiliation of his subjects, for he knows that a mean-spirited man will not conspire against anybody; (2) the creation of mutual mistrust among them, for a tyrant is not overthrown until men begin to have confidence in one another. This is why tyrants make war on the good…; (3) the tyrant desires to keep his subjects incapable of action, for no one attempts what is impossible, and they will not attempt to overthrow his tyranny, if they are powerless (373).

By contrast, in Book VI he begins chapter 2 with an assertion that "the basis of a democratic state is liberty, which, according to the common opinion of men, can be enjoyed only in such a state. This they affirm to be the great end of every democracy" (379). Two qualities that accompany such a state, which I will not pursue but only mention, are education and leisure (406, 413).

Both Plato and Aristotle transmit strong fantasies of what constitutes a virtuous person and, by extension, a city or society that mirrors such an individual's vitality. What both reveal as well is the intricate relationship between individual, social structure, ethos of place, as well as education's seminal role in creating a politically fair and socially just atmosphere, in which every citizen may breathe freely the air of opportunity.

Contemporary Variations

I end this aspect of the discussion with a more contemporary voice. Avishai Margalit, Professor Emeritus of Philosophy at the Hebrew University in Jerusalem's recent book is *The Ethics of Memory*, a superb account of what a society chooses to remember and to forget and from which I have drawn in this essay. But an earlier study is more poignant at this juncture: *The Decent Society*. In it he exposes how a decent society, to put it simply here, is one whose institutions do not humiliate people. His insight is profound in its simplicity. He furthers his discussion by comparing a decent society to a civilized one. The latter "is a microethical concept concerned with the relationships between individuals, while the idea of a decent society is a macroethical concept concerned with the setup of the society as a whole" (2). Self-respect, not self-esteem, is the appropriate goal of honor, he claims, because "self-respect is independent of any action or omission by other people toward one…" (11).

It seems to me that a politically healthy philosophy allows for the conjunction "and" that resides between politics—American or otherwise—and social justice. Not versus or "as opposed to," but "and." Not opposition but apposition. A real quantum leap would be to reach a point where the "and" is no longer needed, where it seeks effacement, wherein a political philosophy and a vital sense of justice fold into one another. Merton is helpful here as he addresses in "Christianity and Totalitarianism" the tendency to confuse faith and prejudice:

> Faith and prejudice have a common need to rely on authority and in this they can sometimes be confused by one who does not understand their true nature. But faith rests on the authority of love while prejudice rests on the pseudo-authority of hatred. (*Disputed Questions* 132)

Thirteen Ways of Looking at a Paradox

I end this brief discussion with a series of counterpoints between U.S. Politics and Social Justice as I understand these massive terms, both in their lived reality and in their ideal condition:

1. United States politics appears increasingly acerbic and feeds on a single diet of competition and sinister complicity. Social justice bends more toward cooperation and compromise.
2. U.S. politics is more narcissistic and self-aggrandizing. Social justice tends toward an authentic generosity of spirit.
3. U.S. politics seems to delight in waste and fiscal and philosophical incontinence. Its mainstay diet is a bloated budget. Social justice must tend towards thrift and gift.
4. U.S. politics allows a free play of lobbying for selfish ends, graft, nepotism and self-promotion. Social justice is based on a form of gifting, of giving, in a largesse of spirit that concentrates on the Common Good.

5. U.S. politics seems bent on self-serving and protecting its own fantasies that harbor and preserve its wounded condition. Social justice is based on a selfless yielding to the needs of others without an agenda-driven self-absorption.
6. U.S. politics rests on forgetting and ignoring the past, compelled rather to forge always the new, the novel, which appears as it unfolds as more of the safe and familiar. Social justice is based on remembrance, recollection and retrieval of a good that allows the greatest number to benefit.
7. U.S. politics has as its foundation a general absence of courage and an inordinate amount of fear of loss of position and security. Social justice rests on courageous and expansive consciousness.
8. U.S. politics appears pockmarked by scandals that demean the spirit of democracy's nobility as outlined initially by early Greek philosophy. Social justice revisions a sacred quality of being and values the whole within which the individual participates to the extent of one's talents and capacities.
9. U.S. politics struggles to exclude and protect the insider. Social justice wrestles to in-corporate inclusively.
10. U.S. politics carries within it a pseudo-epic but authentic tragic cast. Social justice is inspired by an authentic epic and a comic cast.
11. U.S. politics has become enslaved as a lowly servant to the myth of capitalism, to which it has capitulated. Social justice must bring capitalistic impulses to serve its goals of equality and fair play.
12. U.S. politics feeds on bi-partisan acrimony and fragmentation. Social justice strives to unify, coalesce and integrate the noblest qualities of the human soul.
13. U.S. politics is enamored of a gilded age, a surface glow. Social justice struggles to recollect and make present a golden age.

While each cultural artifact—politics and justice—carries a shadow of itself and must therefore be vigilant of its own destructive tendencies, each deploys as well a nobility of soul that has been deleted from the current restricted conversation. A stingy and narrow way of speaking of both dimensions has crept into the field. The first step to renewing and reinvigorating the qualities of politics and justice is to seek a wider vocabulary, a more vibrant lexicon, fresh metaphors, revived symbols, a reinvigorated imagination of inclusion, in which these ideas and ideals may be transformed in a vessel worthy of their existence. The logos of a people is the vessel in which that same people's mythos flourishes or languishes.

Works Cited

Aristotle. *Politics.* In Loomis, L.R. (Ed). *Aristotle: On Man In the Universe.* Trans. Benjamin Jowett. New York: Gramercy Books, 1943. 246-416.

Campbell, Joseph. *Thou Art That: Transforming Religious Metaphor.* Ed. Eugene Kennedy. Novato, California: New World Library, 2001.

Havel, Vaclav. *The Art of the Impossible: Politics as Morality in Practice. Speeches and Writings, 1990-1996.* Trans. Paul Wilson and others. New York: Fromm International, 1997.

Kean, Thomas H. and Hamilton, Lee H. *The 9/11 Commission Report: Authorized Edition.* New York: W.W. Norton and Company, 2003.

Margalit, Avishai. *The Decent Society.* Trans. Naomi Goldblum. Cambridge: Harvard UP, 1998.

Merton, Thomas. *Conjectures of a Guilty Bystander.* New York: Doubleday, 1989.

---. *Disputed Questions.* San Diego: Harcourt Brace, 1980.

Plato. *Republic.* In Hamilton, E. and H. Cairns (Eds.). *Plato: The Collected Dialogues, Including the Letters.* Trans. Paul Shorey. Bollingen Series LXXI. Princeton: Princeton UP, 1973. 575-845.

---. *Laws.* In Hamilton, E. and H. Cairns (Eds.). *Plato: The Collected Dialogues, Including the Letters.* Trans. A.E. Taylor. Bollingen Series LXXI. Princeton: Princeton UP, 1973. 1225-1516.

CHAPTER 3

DANTE'S *TERZA RIMA* IN *THE DIVINE COMEDY*: THE ROAD OF THERAPY

Love and the gracious heart are but one thing, /as
that wise poet puts it in his poem; /as much can one
without the other be/ as without reason can the
reasoning mind.
~Dante, *La Vita Nuova* 39

The pursuit of gnosis seems a perennial desire of being human
and feeling that fire of desire in the belly to gain greater
consciousness. Perhaps *knowing*, a present participle and a gerund, is
both an action from the verb and a condition from the noun. As a
part of speech, gerunds may comprise the linguistic structure of the
new physics because of their ability to include at once both
movement and matter. As such, present participles not only represent
a part of speech, but more to the concerns of this essay, may indeed
be archetypes of rhetoric because they allow something like knowing
to be both an action and a state of being, which encourages a new

pattern of awareness, as in the following two sentences:

> Knowing that Italy would be warm in July, Sandy packed several sleeveless blouses.

In this structure *knowing* is an action. But a crucial shift occurs in the second sentence:

> Knowing is one corridor that may lead to wisdom.

Here in the same word, but strolling now in a new neighborhood, *knowing* is a condition of being.

To pursue what may be archetypally resolute about wisdom traditions invites a few earlier questions: What is knowing? Is there a stream of consciousness that leads from perception to reflection to knowledge to wisdom? Does wisdom abrupt, full blown, when the goddess Athena is deployed in all of her resplendent warrior wisdom from the forehead of her father, Zeus, as an icon for consciousness itself? The Spanish philosopher, Jose Ortega y Gasset, calls that condition faced by all human beings, "to have it out with their surroundings...they have to know what to abide by about it" (198). He refers to this condition of figuring out what to believe about one's surroundings the construction of "a primordial reality" which is "to set in motion their intellectual apparatus, the main organ of which—I contend—is the imagination" (198).

Is there inherent, therefore, in the nature and indeed the structure of poetic knowledge, an organizing principle that offers a particular angle of vision on wisdom as part of a poetic tradition? My thesis here is that poetry is *mimetic* precisely because psyche is analogic, metaphoric and mythic in both its posturings as verb and as noun. We could, with some reward, open psyche up to a discussion of adjectives, pronouns, prepositions, even the psycho-dynamics of commas and semicolons, but that is another essay on psyche's grammatical proclivities.

By asserting the above observation, I want to create a short but richly endowed pearl necklace, the beads of which include Aristotle, Dante and C.G. Jung, in that historical order, but not necessarily in that same mythic beadwork. The reclusive and profound poet of New England, Emily Dickinson, gathers so much of what will be explored here in one of her most pithy poetic pronouncements:

> Tell all the Truth—but tell it slant,
> Success in Circuit lies;
> Too bright for our infirm Delight
> The Truth's superb surprise.
> As Lightning to the Children eased,
> With explanation kind
> The truth must dazzle gradually,
> Or every man be blind—(#1129, 506-07)

The truth must be grazed, perhaps leaving a discernible burn mark on the exposed arm as it passes intimately by; it must not be assaulted directly from front or behind; rather, it must be taken in subtly, with nuance aforethought. So might the same be said for wisdom itself. The slant part of telling the truth is a poetic move because it suggests that the major vehicle to carry the tenor of truth is metaphor and analogy, both eager presenting symptoms that encourage indirection to find direction out, which the obsequious Polonius suggests to his son Laertes' friend, Reynaldo during the early warning storms of deceit in Shakespeare's *Hamlet.*

Moreover, my sense is that metaphorical knowing is archetypal, what Jung himself called an archetype of transformation. In *The Archetypes and the Collective Unconscious*, his first chapter is devoted to outlining the physiology of archetypes. As he nears the end of an in-depth discussion of three archetypal figures—the shadow, the anima and the wise old man—figures which he believes "can be directly experienced in personified form" (*Collected Works* $9_{,1}$ ¶80), he decides to include, in what feels almost like an after-thought, another brand of archetype, what he refers to as "*archetypes of transformation.*" They are not personalities, he insists, but are rather akin to typical situations, places, ways and means, that symbolize the kind of transformation in question.... They are genuine symbols because they are ambiguous, full of half-glimpsed meanings, and in the last resort, inexhaustible" (*CW* $9_{,1}$ ¶80).

Symbolic reality then, if we extend Jung's insight, is a valid and perennial way both of knowing and of seeking wisdom. Symbols, like metaphors, which the mythologist Joseph Campbell called "the native tongue of myth" (*Flight* 8), includes as well similes, correspondences, analogies, all of which offer pathways to wisdom through knowledge that is figural in their intention, indirect in their focus and yet precise in their structure. The importance of such power to direct the soul towards knowledge and wisdom Campbell corrals in the following assertion: "The life of a mythology springs from and depends on the metaphoric vigor of its symbols" (6). By the rich word *vigor* I understand him to mean it must contain enough psychic libidinal energy to further the knowledge contained therein. Like a particularly powerful dream, it must amass enough energy to break through into conscious awareness and settle with surety in the memory. When a metaphor, or even an entire mythos, loses vigor, it collapses like a wet rag into a personal or cultural cliché.

Knowing, in addition, is by indirection, one of the hallmarks of poetic intuition or instinct, what I choose to call a *gnosopoetics* or *mythopoetics,* for it requires something to be taken in by perception, imagined anew, ordered in its content and then articulated through some medium of coherence to form a complete experience. Not meaning but an experience of life itself is what Campbell believed people sought in their lives. Meaning is often overrated while life itself remains on the shelf, in the back, unlived and perhaps *underrated.*

Moreover, the physicist and educator, Donald Cowan, informs us in *Unbinding Prometheus: Education for the Coming Age,* that fundamentally learning occurs in three moments: 1. an apprehension or *grasping;* 2. a *mapping;* and 3. a *making* something from the previous two moments (85, my emphasis). This last condition activates *poiesis,* what the philosopher Aristotle referred to as a making or a shaping into a coherent form what had hitherto been untended and unexpressed. Knowledge grows directly from such a process, a pilgrimage of sorts, through just such an imaginal working. It carries with it a tendency to cultivate, a tending, as one does to a field of crops and as such, is intimately connected with culture, for culture itself is a consequence and a product of cultivating, as the philosopher, poet and Kentucky farmer, Wendell Berry articulates so elegantly in *The Unsettling of America: Culture and Agriculture* (43). A fully vibrant culture, it seems to me, is one which cultivates the soil of wisdom herself; wisdom is indeed soiled, sacred and of the earth.

In his *Poetics,* if we leave Jung and poetry for a moment and return to 5th century BCE Athens, Aristotle makes a profound discovery when he explores in detail Sophocles' *Oedipus Rex* as a paradigm for the genre of tragedy and as a fitting launchpad for remarks on poetry's general nature. In what may be perhaps the first work of literary theory in the West, Aristotle sets out in rather rigid prose to catalogue and differentiate the parts of tragedy as drama. In his exploration, however, I believe he anticipates some major insights of depth psychology, hence his inclusion here. He founds his sense of imitation in pleasure, the kind of pleasure a child experiences by mimicking or imitating, often in exhaustive repetition, some action in play: "For the process of imitation is natural to mankind from childhood on: Man is differentiated from other animals because he is the most imitative of them, and he learns his first lessons through imitation" (*Aristotle's Poetics* 7). I want to set in motion here, but not extend it, a relevant connection between repetition and the more subtle recursivity of psyche's perennial motion to return, to retrieve and to renew what already enjoys a certain familiar domicile in memory. The spiral, then, and not the circle, is the geometry of the soul. My last observation here serves as a brief prolegomena to Dante's *Commedia*, written early in the 14th century, which will enter this discussion momentarily.

Learning is a pleasurable act, Aristotle continues. It grows from "viewing representations because it turns out that they learn and infer what each thing is—for example, that this particular object is that kind of object" (7). Knowing by analogy gives pleasure, if not joy, in the act of learning. To think, remember and articulate by analogy is joy-full because it affords pleasure in the act of creating one-in-relationship to what may be unfamiliar, and then successfully yoking it to the familiar. The heartbeat of poetry throbs right here, as does the pleasure which accrues from such a sustained blood pressure.

Aristotle suggests this is an inborn impulse; perhaps like an instinct it has its corollary in the archetypal realm of psyche and in an archetypal "ways and means" of Jung's definition of *archetypes of transformation* cited earlier. Poetry, and here tragedy specifically in Aristotle's calculus, imitates an action, "not of men, but of life, for life consists in action" (8). Not only is this action the origin of poetry, it is the origin of learning itself. I further assert that it is the origin of archetypes and of their study in archetypal psychology, their aesthetic presence in art and poetry, and the origin of the road to wisdom. Such an action resides at the center of therapy itself and may constitute a central gesture in all healing.

I say this because of a dependent adverbial clause of Jung's that arrested me years ago, and which I contend carries the payload inherent in depth psychology. I cite it here from *Aion: Researches into the Phenomenology of the Self*: "Since analogy formation is a law which to a large extent governs the life of the psyche…" (*CW* 9,₂ ¶414). I sidestep the main clause of this sentence; it is not needed for my purposes here. But I do believe this dependent clause is worth a moment of meditation for what it implies.

In this clause Jung is Aristotelian in a very specific way: both Aristotle and Jung share a belief that innate to the human being is an impulse towards analogy formation, or an instinct to imitate by discovering similarities within differences. Advertising knows this implicitly and any successful marketing campaign is predicated on this core insight. Both Aristotle and Jung share as well a similar sense of the power of analogy's presence as a way of knowing. The subtle slide from knowledge is yet to be explored. Analogy, moreover, is the cloak worn by symbol, metaphor, simile and myth, often of a brightly colored fabric.

Let's add Joseph Campbell to the discussion in order to reveal his connection to both Aristotle and Jung. He insists at the end of the first chapter of *Thou Art That*: "A system of mythological symbols only works if it operates in the field of a community of people who have essentially analogous experiences, or to put it another way, if they share the same realm of life experience" (8). Not duplicate lives, but the same realm, which allows sufficient latitude for one to achieve an original journey in this sublunary territory.

In our story, *plot* for Aristotle, is the soul of tragedy (*Poetics* 13) and we could add, the soul of poetry; character is second in importance, for character is the vehicle that carries the tenor of the plot. Tragedy, Aristotle further asserts, "is an imitation of an action; and it is, on account of this, an imitation of men acting" (13). Francis Fergusson, commenting on the word *action* in his own edited volume of the *Poetics*, believes it is not overt action, but rather, citing Dante, whom we will welcome in a moment, "a movement of spirit" and even that is invisible but no less real and takes place *sub rosa*, in the realm of the invisible movement of psyche. Fergusson cites the theorist, S.H. Butcher's definition of this action: "The praxis that art seeks to reproduce is mainly a *psychic energy* working outwards" (qtd. in Fergusson 8, my emphasis). Finally, the philosopher Paul Ricoeur's in-depth work on mimesis yields this observation: "mimesis performs the same kind of guiding-concept function for poetry that persuasion does for prose in the public arena" (36). Poetry and prose both persuade with a force that while shared is not identical. Their energy valences are quite different but not unrelated.

To say we are "moved" by a film, a story, a painting, or a piece of music, even a personal memory, or that we feel the power of a poem or an image, is to be mimetically engaged in something profound and transpersonal being imitated in our own being that resonates and mirrors the plot or soul of the work's movement even while it sparks a vague intuitive knowing within us. Dualistic responses that split self from world, spirit from matter and soul from mimetic art—all collapse here under the weight of imaginal involvement. In an insightful "Foreword" to a recent book on Jung and Henry Corbin, *Green Man, Earth Angel* by Tom Cheetham, spiritual psychologist Robert Sardello calls this form of perception "subjectively-objective," wherein in an "imaginal metaphysics all dualism is resolved so that there is no longer a subject-object distinction; rather, subject and object are one" (xv). Dante's *Commedia* reflects, as a poetic artifact, such a collapse or resolution by deploying the reader into the actual pilgrimage of the poet who recollects that experience. By extension, moreover, the reader is cast upon the story of his/her own growth into consciousness, realized in the pilgrimage of reading and imagining Dante's own fabricated journey.

Mythopoiesis, then, includes not just the creation of the work of art, but the way in which the myth inherent in the work is reshaped in our own imagination by this universal mimetic faculty or capacity to imagine. Wisdom, archetypal wisdom, is spawned in just this mythic backwater through the sluice of imaginal knowing. One important implication here is that psyche is fundamentally aesthetic, that *aesthesis* is its ground of being, its fundamental ontology.

Let me conjecture at this juncture, a metaphor:

> Plot is to character
> as
> Action is to wisdom.

The first part of the metaphor—plot is to character—is the embodied, incarnate and perceivable reality. But underneath the hood beats the engine of action/wisdom, the power source that, like a poetic delivery system, offers plot-character both its energy and its motion—even its motivation. Moreover, under this same hood resides the intensity of vigor that, as Campbell reminds us, the metaphor must contain if it is to unleash the energy necessary to both raise and shape consciousness and with it, perception. Here resides the words of O.B. Hardison, scholar and commentator of the *Poetics*. In discussing Aristotle's critical apparatus, he springs forward in time to the neo-platonist Plotinus (204-70 AD). Hardison interprets Plotinus' understanding of *nous* as "a creative force seeking to emanate outward, to fill all possible gaps in the scale of being, and to realize itself in material creation" (282). John Dillon in "The Extracts from the First Edition" of *The Enneads* calls *nous* "Divine Mind" or "Divine Intellection" (xxxiii).

The poet begins to take shape here (this is my abiding hope) as a divinely-chosen individual, one numinously-inspired, not as Plato would promote, one who creates falsehoods, illusions and wretched simulacra of the *Truth*, a word Dickinson's poem earlier encouraged us to consider. What the poet creates is "charged with divine *energia* and . . . has a priest-like function of revealing truth to men's clouded vision" (Hardison 283). One key corridor into such a revelation, Hardison insists, is by imitating the world through "looking to their divine archetypes and producing images of them as they might or ought to be" (284). His thought is in line not only with Jung's but with the profound meditations of anthropologist Robert Plant Armstrong in *The Powers of Presence*.

Writing in the same imaginal furrows as the above two thinkers, Armstrong diligently develops in a beautiful and complex way the idea that all works of art carry or embody a force or presence which "tend to gratify the human psyche" (4). Briefly, works which carry the power of "affecting presence" have a certain *mana* personality about them: "they are special kinds of things ('works') which have significances not primarily conceptual (they are 'affecting'), and which own certain characteristics that cause them to be treated more like persons than like things ('presence')" (5). Moreover, like persons, they "exist in a state of ambiguity" (5). Yet they also carry the status of a thing, so they are both subjective and objective. "In fact, 'power' seems the most appropriate name for those distinctive though elusive properties.... It is power which quickens us so that we greatly prize such things and, thus, so universally make them" (6). Through the powers of affecting presence, things have the capacity to assume mythic qualities, which once again implicate vigor, power and energy: "These universal, generative energies and states are 'mythologems' (a word I borrow from Jung, who uses it to mean 'archetype'), and they occur in fairly stable form from people to people" (Armstrong 48-49).

From this weaving of the various voices collating the different energy sources, I discern that without contact with the myth in the matter, wisdom remains ever-elusive. Wisdom in some manner or condition resides in the ability of the energy innate in affective presence to work on us, to shape us poetically as we imagine the work. Of course, the relationship is reciprocal: what are the effects of my own affective presence on the work of art? A longer exploration of reading as an alchemical act of the soul is needed on just this topic.

The discussion grows even richer when we remember that etymologically, the word *plot* translates as *muthos,* and for Aristotle the plot must follow "the inner logic of poetic art" (*Aristotle* 31). In other words, present is an organizing principle at work in the plot, which I suspect finds its correspondence in the *inner logos* of the audience members. Active, therefore, is an interior logos in the plot that finds its analogies in the guiding mythos of each individual. Mythos, therefore, is an invisible inner logos, as a visible analogy of a deeper mystery that mythos taps, provokes and joyfully incites. The plot of a work of art is then both a content and an action, since each of our lives shuttles between noun and verb. The plot itself, then, is the aperture into wisdom, gleaned through the deeper reservoir of the action, a basin of the mythologems.

I understand now how Plotinus himself can ask in the Seventh Tractate: "Is There an Ideal Archetype of Particular Beings?" which is the title of his very short chapter (406-09) of *The Enneads*, which in this Tractate, rests on a principle of doubling and analogy. Plotinus puts forth the idea that each of us has a Soul which "contains the Reason-Principles of all that it traverses, [then] once more all men have their (archetypic) existence" (406-07). Not only is this so, but he further suggests that "every soul contains all the Reason-Principles that exist in the Cosmos: since the Cosmos contains the Reason-Principles not merely of man, but also for all individual living things, so must the Soul" (407). He tells us clearly, lest we become confused over the term "Soul," that for him it means "principle of Life" (409).

This very principle of life is the fuel for the engine of mimesis in poetry itself. Aristotle, if I grasp at all Stephen Halliwell's excursus on the nature of imitation (mimesis), as well as the structure of poetic unity, tends us closer to the poetic wisdom, archetypally-grounded and psychologically-oriented, that sets the stage for the pilgrim-poet Dante's life's journey both as pilgrim and as poet in the *Commedia*.

If poetry is an imitation of an action that must through its plot, represent one complete action "whole and complete and of a certain magnitude" (Halliwell 14), as Aristotle insists, then some imaginal dance must arise between the world we know and the world that poetry makes visible—and most crucially, *possible*—to our discerning aesthetic gaze. Here Halliwell is very helpful: "the events of a dramatic poem should exhibit a higher intelligibility, particularly *causal* intelligibility, than is usually to be found in life" (135). He further argues that "the plot of a dramatic poem, which is its essential structure of action, is not to be understood as simply corresponding to reality past or present…but as representing a heightened and notional *pattern of possibility*, and as therefore more accessible to rational apprehension than are the events of ordinary experience" (135, italics mine). Let's pause for a moment on the phrase "representing a heightened and notional pattern of possibility." Aristotle suggests through Halliwell's interpretation that poetry contains or perhaps *is*, an aesthetic expression of a more deeply intuited pattern of psyche that may just establish a power of *affecting presence*. More time would prompt me right here to develop how this last sentence conveys the genesis of one's personal mythos.

Nonetheless, I believe this notional pattern of possibility is the realm of the archetypal. Unless the poem generates sufficient "wisdom energy," it does not have the *sforza*, as Italians label it, or the strength, the Eros, or the libidinal power to shape our imaginations into an awareness of this "pattern of possibility." Therefore, in its proportions and in its expression of a single action that itself is whole and complete, it inaugurates a certain joy in witnessing it because it aesthetically delights the senses, the intellect and the emotions, as well as the more collective archetypal level imbedded in the specific action. Moreover, at least in any discussion of poetry and wisdom derived therefrom, one that inclines towards Aristotle, the apprehension of beauty is part of this experience. Aesthetics itself has its own hydraulics, its own turbines of energy, to extend the metaphor a bit.

To achieve it, however, perhaps on the first, the fourth, the fifteenth reading, is to gain wisdom inherent in the action. The biologist Brian Goodwin reminds us that "Ideas have their time, and if you happen to discover something before people are ready to recognize its significance, you might as well leave it in the bottom drawer until the climate is receptive" (46). So with a deepening mimetic understanding of a poem: it has its own time to reveal itself. Mimesis is achieved on some level, determined of course by our growing capacity to discern this pattern of possibility. We are speaking less of content than of coherence, discerned, wisely enough, from an expanded and deepened awareness of the work's action. Not its message, not its meaning, not its character development, but its internal form is most relevant to shape matter into meaning through a lived experience.

To touch this formative principle by the fingertips of our imaginal involvement is the goal of the reading—itself a complex pilgrimage through the poem's lush or austere landscape—as well as by apprehending at least a fraction of its generic form. Now all of the above is in service of getting us to Halliwell's final insight:

> It is not immediately to life that the poet must turn for his material, but to an imagined world (including that of inherited myth) in which the underlying designs of causality, so often obscured in the world as we encounter it, will be made manifest. (135)

By turning to myth, I suspect, the poet reshapes and reforms the lineaments and contours of it to suit his/her vision of patterned possibilities (general) by means of the specific plot, wherein characters interact, think, feel and react to their surroundings and to one another (particular). The general or universal or archetypal action is thus embedded squarely in the particular sinews of the concrete narrative.

The reader then experiences deeply in his/her soul the imagined world in the making—what I would term a *mytho-poetic* achievement of consciousness. To enter such a realm is to know, to come to a knowledge unavailable any other way or through any other disciplines. Poetic knowledge is its own form of ontological awareness. It deepens and expands, even makes elastic, our own limited world view. It does so, not by trying to match its reality to the one we swim in daily, but by creating an imagined form of a reality that exists only in the poem. Not sociology, politics, theology or political correctness but *poiesis* is what the poet seeks to imagine into a formed experience.

The *Commedia's* Force Field: *Terza Rima*

The depth psychologist Michael Conforti has explored the self-organizing dynamics in the natural order in *Field, Form and Fate*, recently reissued by Spring Journal Publications (2003). He begins in that study by deploying, in part, Jung's analogy between the nature of the archetype and "the axial system of a crystal which determines the crystalline structure in the liquid, although it has no material existence of its own" (*CW* $9_{,1}$ ¶155). The analogy here in poetry is the substance of the form of a poem. I remember reading this comparison for the first time and being moved to assent to the wisdom inherent in its power.

My intention in this essay is to suggest that a similar action occurs between the nature of the archetype and the axial system of a poem, such as Dante's, within the imaginal life of the reader, a pilgrim companion in the act of reading, and no less analogous to Dante's voyage as pilgrim, and his second pilgrimage as writer of the voyage we, he assumes, have signed on and submitted to.

I wish less to interpret the almost incomprehensively brilliant content of this poem but to reside and dwell instead in its rhythmic and constant dance pattern: the *terza rima*. Dante, scholars assert, invented such a rhyme scheme for this poem, written between 1310-1313; he then backfilled its plot to 1300 to assure that his prophetic pronouncements would enjoy a certain historical veracity. I underscore or place in italics the pattern of the poem's rhyme scheme, for in it, of course married to the content of the lines, is a pattern of wisdom, if such a property is possible, both of learning and of therapeutic healing. I am indebted to the last chapter of the Dante scholar, John Freccero's superb study, *Dante: The Poetics of Conversion*, for introducing me to the subtle motions of the poem's patterned canzone.

At the outset I suggest that the *terza rima* is an archetype of transformation; to be transformed is predicated on being in motion. *Terza rima* is both noun and verb. Much more can be said of the tri-partite or trinitarian structure of the entire poem; however, my goal is to explore just this rhyme scheme in its triune structure. As a structure and an action it is as well a gerund in its dramatic role in the poem. Perhaps therapy itself must be willing to oscillate between the noun and verb forms of the psyche.

The entire 100 cantos of Dante's *Commedia* relate in memory the plot, or *muthos,* of one soul waking in a dark wood to recognize that he has lost the path of his life, his connection to himself and to any allegiance or presence of the divine. In short, he has stepped out of the coherent mythos that gives meaning and coherence to life. The recoil from such a move is sudden homelessness in the world. Almost immediately, and spurred by fear, he attempts the hero's journey on his own but is quickly rebuffed by three beasts who confront him; they can be understood as figures of Dante's own excessive appetites. With the help of three primary guides and mentors recruited by the Blessed Virgin, Mary, do the classical poet Virgil, the lovely and forceful historical figure of Beatrice Portinari, and the holy figure of Bernard of Clairveax, help the pilgrim confront the paradox of his final vision. Each figure assists him differently on his therapeutic journey towards wholeness.

In the course of his pilgrimage deep into the offal of Inferno, up into the wounding, then cleansing habitation of Mount Purgatory, and finally through the celestial highways of the planets to the Primum Mobile in Paradiso, Dante meets, argues with, feels pity for, chastises and loves an entire population of figures that colonize variously myth, poetry and history. The poem is, among other things, the richest and most detailed exemplum of what Joseph Campbell discovered was inherent in so many mythologies world-wide: the hero's struggle to enter the woods of unknowing, to confront oppositions and aids, to engage in conflict with the adversarial parts of oneself, and to return to his/her community with the boon of new knowledge, indexed and catalogued now under "M" for *mystical wisdom narrative.*

To tell his story, Dante adapts the rhythmic rhyme scheme of *terza rima* in which three lines, akin to the poem's footsteps, or footprints, detail the motion of the poem and our involvement in both its sustained rhythm and content. Let us look at the first examples of this structure in *Inferno* 1 that begins with these lines:

> Nel mezzo del cammin di nostra vita **A**
> mi ritrovai per una selva oscura, **B**
> che la dirritta via era smarrita. **A**
> Ahi quanto a dir qual era e cosa dura **B**
> esta selva selvaggia e aspra e forte **C**
> che nel pensier rinova la paura! **B**
> Tant' e amara che poco e piu morte; **C**
> ma per trattar del ben ch'I' vi trovai, **D**
> diro de l'altre cose ch'I v v'ho scorte. **C**
> Io non so ben ridir com' I' v'intrai, **D**
> tant era pien di sonno a quell punto **E**
> che la verace via abbandonai. **D** (*Inferno* 1. 1-12)

Allen Mandelbaum's translation follows:

> (When I had journeyed half of our life's way,
> I found myself within a shadowed forest,
> for I had lost the path that does not stray.
> Ah, it is hard to speak of what it was,
> that savage forest, dense and difficult,
> which even in recall renews my fear:
> so bitter—death is hardly more severe!
> But to retell the good discovered there,
> I'll also tell the other things I saw.
> I cannot clearly say how I had entered
> the wood; I was so full of sleep just at
> the point where I abandoned the truth path).

Dante has entered as awakened pilgrim the wisdom pathway which he now relates to us in the residue of memory through narrative. That the poem begins midway carries a reflection in the middle term of the *terza rima*. Form and content cannot be separated; knowing grows, I believe, from the interstices, the *metaxes* of the rhyme scheme, and the rhythm of each line's syllables, which remains more or less consistent throughout, the conversation that ensues between cantos that precede and follow the one being read.

Indeed, perhaps the current cliché that life's progress is often comprised of two steps forward and one step back was born here, in the rhyme scheme. But as with most clichés, it skips across the surface of what treasures might dwell in a lower layer. The movement of this scheme, moreover, is for one thing the motion of psyche herself as she seeks understanding and indeed, wisdom. *Terza rima* is psyche's rhythm, its method, its scheme, for knowing; its repetition of rhymed words suggests it is a patterned knowing, a duplicative knowing in fact, wherein some insight is mirrored both backward and forward and gains in the motion a texture and profundity that rests on imitation and remembrance. The rhythm is based, moreover, on what Freccero installs as a constant "recapitulation" (263). Again, the spiral, not the circle is the sacred geometry of the soul always in tension between its history, its presentness and its anticipated futurity.

Consider first the forward movement of A to B. But at this step in the pilgrimage forward, something happens to return one to A that in the word that ends the line at the same instant rhymes with but is not identical to, or an exact copy, of the original A. Not a repetition compulsion is active here but a retreat back into something familiar as well as a step into newness. What is crucial to see is the simultaneous motion into the familiar and unfamiliar at once. The dramatic genius of this structure is that the familiar is new and what newness sprouts here in the retreat to the original rhyme is indeed familiar territory. The second A therefore completes the first "foot" of the terza rima, yet it is and is not the first A. What has intervened to interrupt the two A's not being duplicates is of course, the middle term: B. What the middle term signifies will be suggested in a moment. Nevertheless, we can venture that intervention of the new term saves the similar but not identical terms from rigidifying into a trap of repetition, entrapment and loss of motion in a shuttling rhythm that is a constant recapitulation into new ground.

Nor is it the first A even if the word *vita* was repeated in the second A such that the first *terza rima* would then read *vita, oscura, vita* (instead of *smarrita*), because something crucial has intervened: temporality has entered, specifically in the form of history itself, in the presence of B (*oscura*). Between the forward movements—a two step—and the backward motion—a one step, history erupts into presence as a specific modality of temporality, both in the motion of the body's movement in the pilgrimage and in the motion of the poem's movement in the language. History itself becomes a way of knowing—both personal memory or biography and a larger vessel of history itself. Not just Dante's own personal memory and biography, but history itself, both as a structure for understanding the great patterns that appear to govern human life collectively, and as the specific cultural history of his own era.

Such is Dante's archetypal genius: to wed *poiesis* (imagination's shaping capacity) to history, perception to memory, body to spirit, and motion to myth. I include this last term because in the language of the poem, what has been first experienced as a literal event—the journey through inferno, purgatory and paradise—is now recollected. But this recollection is also a new form, a fresh telling or expression of the original journey. It is more a recollection deeply imagined for its further possibilities. Therefore it is a recollection in hope. The journey has taken on mythic proportions, or better said, *mytho-poetic* proportions in the recollection that is also an imaginal motion forward. I should note as well that in this microcosm of the *terza rima* is the complex journey of the hero as Campbell adumbrates it repeatedly in his writings, but most fully in *The Hero with a Thousand Faces* (49-244).

Therapy as *Terza-Rimic* Motion of Soul

The meaning of the poem, but only after the experience of the journey that is its content and structure, stirs to the surface like sea life from fathomless depths, through the oscillating rhythm of the rhyme scheme. Structure is archetypal and yields its own form of knowing; it connects intimately with the movement or rhythm of the reader-pilgrim-interpreter that is the poem's trinitarian audience. The poem's wisdom stretches out in sympathy to meet the reader's own psychic rhythm; we learn, the poem seems to insist, by recollecting into newness. I say this with one eye on the rhyme scheme:

A------B------A
to
B------C------B

So that

> The first B *(oscura)*, the middle term of the first *terza rima*
>   becomes
> B *(dura)*---C (forte)---B *(paura!)*

The middle term of the preceding *terza rima* metamorphoses into the first and last rhymes of the next *terza rima*. In that transformation, moreover, what do we discern and experience as readers?

Memory herself in the figure of the Greek goddess, Mnemosyne, stirs the heart's vessel of forward motion, of breaking into new ground, or seeing anew by means of what has just passed. Now the past is retrieved into new envisionings. If we pull the lens back just a bit for a moment, we as pilgrim-readers (and it appears that all deep reading is a pilgrimage of memory wedded to imagination), we do sense that the first *terza rima* deals with the past—"I found," "I had lost"—the next with the present—"it is hard to speak of what it was"—as it unfolds, unfurls, curls or spirals back into the past—"which even in recall renews my fear" (che nel pensier rinova la paura!)—and the third envelops the future—"But to retell the good discovered there/I'll also tell the other things I saw"—which wraps past/present/future into a tightly corded knot of omni-temporal meaning. My own sense is that in therapy, all three dimensions must be operative, provoked, evoked so that the entire person as client is present in his/her past-future being.

Such complexity, to thicken the baroque quality of the poem's structure further, is braided into another figure, one that Freccero discerns in this manner: "The geometric representation of forward motion which is at the same time recapitulatory is the spiral" (263). Therefore, the reader must assuredly tread this poem wearing non-skid hiking boots, for he/she is going to be asked to traverse tough terrain with often cantankerous talus slipping under one's feet; to move backward and forward in the *terza rima* rhythm, and to spiral down, then up, through the first 67 cantiche that comprise the Infernal and Purgatorial realms, is the dance Dante's poem insists we engage if we are to grasp its moving meanings. A rough and tenuous pilgrimage indeed, not for the faint of heart or the visually unchallenged reader.

Finally, and for the ritual of therapy itself, something that might seem obvious here should not be missed or down-sized: the middle term of the *terza rima* scheme *becomes* the first and last terms of the next step in the poem. Now if we think of the three parts of the foot of *terza rima* comprising past, present, future, and the middle term as present becoming both past and future of the next foot, then the notion of the linear trajectory of past—present—future is an illusion that Dante's poem exposes. In other words, rather than there being a past—present—future, there is only present. There is a present of the past; a present of the present; and a present of the future. *Presencing* is the heart of therapy; the idea that the past is recollected or that the future is anticipated is true with the caveat that it is their presentness that is always exercising its sovereignty, not a past being recollected, but a presencing of the past as well as a presencing of the future. Not linear but rather mythic time is the frame for therapy, for poetry and for increasing one's orbit of being conscious.[1]

The practical application to therapy, and recall that I am not a therapist, would be to assist the client in collapsing the notion that the past is back there and that the future is out there; quite to the contrary: both past and future are imbedded in the middle term of the *terza rima* temporal scheme. One's ability to imagine time differently through the rhyme scheme would elicit, it seems to me, very different responses to one's relation to the story of their past and the trajectory of their future.

Finally, let's allow Jung in on the conversation at this juncture since his insight bears directly on the rhythmic rhyming structure of the poem. In developing his discussion on the qualities of psyche that leads to understanding, Jung centers on intuition, which he understands as a way of feeling: "But intuition, as I conceive it, is one of the basic functions of the psyche, namely, *perception of the possibilities inherent in a situation*" (*Collected Works* 8 ¶292). Implicit in his remark is Dante's *terza rima* structure, at least to this extent: the movement forward from A—B and then a return to A—advances a particular perception based on re-cognition that is much richer than one afforded the pilgrim as he journeys from A to B before retreating back to a new A!

What is gained in this reversal, or backward motion, which both prepares and anticipates another movement forward, is a new horizon of possibilities, what one could not see at first, but sees forward in retrospect. In other words, each step of the *terza rima* opens up its own brand of perception or reflection. A sensibility that there are more possibilities inherent in the situation at any step of the poem's forward thrust is deployed through a greater consciousness when one returns to the first term in the third "moment" of the *terza rimic* unity: A—B—A. The second A is the moment of intuiting what might be possible, based squarely on what has been certain. At every step of the epic pilgrimage, then, certainty consistently collides with uncertainty, clarity with ambiguity, paradox with potentialities, the light of greater understanding with the darkening aspect of the soul's mystery. Such is the psychic rhythm of the poem's organic life throughout the 100 cantos. Such as well is the psychic life of the individual in the therapeutic encounter.

Memory itself, the act of imaginally remembering the future, is the pivot or hinge of the poem's action, exactly marking where the present and the future receive their energy, their direction and their resolve. Memory for the individual reader-pilgrim blossoms out to become history for an entire people, as Freccero traces later in the chapter. What at one moment in time and space is *anticipated*, is in another moment *remembered*, and in another moment *perceived*, so that the dance of *terza rima* is a constant pirouette between past and future with something of the eternal *Now* of the present embodying or incarnating the life force or principle of soul's poetic dynamism.

My sense is that the poem's wisdom is revealed in multiple ways, but here specifically in the rhyme scheme as it weds the content of each three-line foot. What is created in the space of the relation of what is anticipated growing back and down into what is remembered? I suggest it is a metaphorical awareness, a figural and even spiritual sensibility that expands and deepens our capacity for consciousness itself. That Dante makes this abundantly clear in the poem's insistence that one traverse its landscape incarnately, not just intellectually, points us to the primary but not exclusive myth that drives its engines—the incarnation, life, crucifixion and resurrection of Christ as an archetype of the Self.

May not the *terza rima* structure also mirror this mythos—the movement forward into some new event and insight being birthed, grows and develops, suffers, falls back into the past, but is then resurrected—not quite as a recapitulation but as *rejuvenation*? Such is the structure, complex and recursive, of the pilgrimage of life itself, what Aristotle intuited was the real subject matter of poetry mimetically tailored for the audience.

The spirit of rejuvenation through memory, history, mimesis and myth is the constantly oscillating heartbeat, the systole and diastole of the poem. I am not certain where a more profound archetypal wisdom may be found than in the texture and textual structure of such a living, breathing art form that asks each of us to pilgrimage it in his/her own style, in unison with one's own heart rhythm, but always with a certain abandon, so that one is saved from abandoning the true way that is one's destiny, with its origin in the will of He or She who moves and designs all things.

Endnote

[1] I am indebted here to James Olney's work on St. Augustine's *Confessions* and his development of the all-inclusive presence of one's life (Olney 2-11).

Works Cited

Alighieri, Dante *Inferno. The Divine Comedy of Dante Alighieri.* Trans. Allen Mandelbaum. New York: Bantam, 1982.

---. *Vita Nuova.* (Trans. Mark Musa). Oxford, England: Oxford UP, 1992.

Aristotle. *Poetics.* Trans. S.H. Butcher. Intro. Francis Fergusson. New York: Hill and Wang, 1969.

Armstrong, Robert. *The Powers of Presence: Consciousness, Myth and Affecting Presence.* Philadelphia: U Pennsylvania P, 1981.

Berry, Wendell. *The Unsettling of America: Culture and Agriculture.* San Francisco: Sierra Books, 1978.

Campbell, Joseph. *Thou Art That: Transforming Religious Metaphor.* Novato, California: New World Library, 2002.

---. *The Hero With a Thousand Faces.* Bollingen Series XVII. Princeton: Princeton UP, 1973.

---. *The Flight of the Wild Gander: Explorations in the Mythological Dimension. Selected Essays 1944-1968.* Novato, California: New World Library, 2002.

Conforti, Michael. *Field, Form and Fate: Patterns in Mind, Nature and Psyche.* (Rev. Edition). New Orleans: Spring Journal Books, 2003.

Cowan, Donald. *Unbinding Prometheus: Education For the Coming Age.*

Dallas: The Dallas Institute, 1988.

Dickinson, Emily. *The Complete Poems of Emily Dickinson*. Ed. Thomas H. Johnson. New York: Little Brown, 1960.

Freccero, John. *Dante: The Poetics of Conversion*. Cambridge: Harvard UP, 1986.

Goodwin, Brian. (2001). *How the Leopard Changed Its Spots: The Evolution of Complexity*. Princeton: Princeton UP, 2001.

Hardison, O.B. *Aristotle's Poetics*. Trans. Leon Golden. Englewood-Cliffs, New Jersey: Prentice-Hall, 1968.

Halliwell, Stephen. *Aristotle's Poetics*. Chicago: U Chicago P, 1988.

Jung, C.G. *Archetypes of the Collective Unconscious*. In *The Collected Works of C.G. Jung*. Vol. 9,1. Trans. R.F.C. Hull. Princeton: Princeton UP, 1971. 1-41.

---. "On the Nature of the Psyche." In *The Collected Works of C.G. Jung*. Vol. 8. Trans. R.F.C. Hull. Princeton: Princeton UP, 1960. 159-236.

---. "The Structure and Dynamics of the Self." In *The Collected Works of C.G. Jung* Vol. 9,2. Trans. R.F.C. Hull. Princeton: Princeton UP, 1970. 222-265.

Olney, James. *Memory and Narrative: The Weave of Life-Writing*. Chicago: U Chicago P, 1998.

Ortega y Gasset, Jose. *What is Knowledge?* Trans. and ed. Jorge Garcia-Gomez. Albany: SUNY P, 2002.

Plotinus. *The Enneads*. Trans. Stephen MacKenna. New York: Penguin, 1991.

Ricoeur, Paul. *The Rule of Metaphor: Multi-disciplinary Studies of the Creation of Meaning in Language*. Trans. Robert Czerny, Kathleen McLaughlin and John Costello. Toronto: U Toronto P, 1997.

Sardello, Robert. Foreword. In Tom Cheetham, *Green Man, Earth Angel: The Prophetic Tradition and the Battle For the Soul of the World*. Albany: SUNY P, 2005. xi-xvii.

CHAPTER 4

MYSTIC FACES, HISTORY'S TRACES: JOSEPH CAMPBELL, MYSTIC

The Sufi mystic al-Hallaj said the same thing, "I and
my Beloved are one," and he too was crucified. This
is the mystical realization: you and that divine
immortal being of beings of which
you are a particle, are one.
~Joseph Campbell, *Mythic Worlds, Modern Words* 71

Each reader of Joseph Campbell's enormous body of work comes to it seeking what one needs, desires, hopes for or, in some instances, may not expect. I thought that what was going to be the big magnet was what he discerned about myth. I stayed for lunch, to feast on, to my surprise, the mystical quality of his thought, disposition and insights. That is my topic of exploration for this essay. But I also choose to write about him for several reasons that link us, beyond our passion for underlining books as a form of meditation. "Kindred souls" is too kitschy for my tastes; and yet....

Both the Campbell and the Slattery clans have their origins in

County Mayo on the western terrain of southern Ireland. As individuals in those clans, both Campbell and I love to explore that interstitial space that lies moist and shadowy between the realms of spirit, poetry, the depth psychology of C.G. Jung, myth and history. Moreover, we share a love of teaching (I am in my 44th year in the classroom); a sense of humor which shields us from taking ourselves too seriously; a love of language's lyric and metaphoric inflections; a desire to migrate ideas hatched in our reading and teaching to the wider cultural landscape; an openness to travel and to other cultural habits of mind and behavior; a belief, explicit or more understated, that some deep relationship obtains between the mystic and the poet. To this last venue, Joseph Campbell was both.

Campbell added immeasurably to the conversation on world mythology; his major strength as I understand him, is as a magnificent synthesizer and as a harvester of ideas through narrative agglutination. His ability to sum up, to sniff out relationships, to intuit analogies, to create metaphorical bridges between what appear to be disparate cultural expressions, is remarkable, especially when added to his own original insights, adroitly affirmed with both conviction and grace. So often have I gazed at his neat, thin and sharply-penciled hand on yellow legal pads of his work in the Joseph Campbell Archives housed at Pacifica Graduate Institute in Carpinteria, California. He had adopted the habit of summarizing a book in neat bullet points on yellow paper. The curator for the Archives, Richard Buchen, told my students and me that when Campbell finished a book, he would summarize it in one page, a compressed distillation of many pages of neatly-inscribed notes. It is as if he compressed it in order to better comprehend what he had read. Compression and comprehension went hand-in-hand with his thin silver metal ruler, the instrument he used with fidelity during his meditation exercises. It is prominently housed in a glass case in the Archives, reminding one of a crown jewel under glass, or a sliver of the true cross on eternal display for pilgrims to gaze on with reverence and awe. How many miles that ruler covered in lines of print only Campbell could venture a guess.

His own roots are no less compressed. His grandfather, Charles, the Larsens' biography of Campbell informs us, sailed from County Mayo during the three years (1845-47) in which the potato crop failed. Charles married and fathered three children: Mary and

Rebecca and Charles William, who will become Joseph Campbell's father (*Fire in the Mind* 6). Reflecting later on his family's heritage and their living in Boston, Joseph Campbell said that "being an Irish Catholic in Boston or New York in those days . . . was 'to be neither fish nor fowl'" (7).

Early in 1928, when he was 24, his biographers relate, he made his first sojourn to Ireland. His initial quips about his impressions reflect the vernacular speaking that Campbell would be known for throughout his life: "Ireland was a funny little dream," and "My trip to Ireland was a riot" (95). Much later, and now accompanied by his wife, Jean, the two traveled to Ireland in 1957 so he could trace, with great relish, the sacred geography of *Finnegans Wake*, and "to follow the course of the hearse in the *Wake*" (Larsen 433). The land of his heritage assumed a mythopoetic hue as Campbell tracked the mystical, dreamy novel of James Joyce published 4 May, 1939 (*A Skeleton Key to Finnegan's Wake* xiii). Five years later, Campbell, along with Henry Morton Robinson, published *The Skeleton Key* in 1944, which remained for years the only extensive guide to such an innovative and enigmatic fictional labyrinth stewing language, myth, history and pure Irish genius in an original rhetorical/poetic Irish recipe.

Readers of Campbell would not be surprised to learn that Joyce's dream work captured the imagination of the budding mythologist, for the novel carries both a mythos and a mystical linguistic landscape that I believe lies at the heart of Campbell's inclinations as a writer and as a person. To that sensibility, or way of being conscious to and in the world, I wish to devote the remainder of this essay. I hope to reveal some of the lineaments of this propensity for the mystical in and through his involvement with the mythical. Indeed, like Thomas Merton or the Anglican priest, Bede Griffiths, or C.G. Jung, Campbell is both a synthesizer and a unifier of large sweeps of history and culture. His delight lies largely in seeking and discovering patterns inherent in the human soul that find expression in world mythologies and religious traditions, literary patterns and rituals world-wide. His landscape of exploration is global, finding within it inflected (one of his favorite words) local customs and mores of behavior and thought. To that extent, he is an inheritor of a tradition of work begun in 1934 when Maud Bodkin wrote her classic work, *Archetypal Patterns in Poetry* that, she hoped would further unite the studies of "psychology and imaginative literature" (Preface v). Freud and Jung were her two priests of the imagination in this innovative project.

Perhaps a salient place to begin is with an observation of Campbell's in *Oriental Mythology*, the second volume of his magnum opus, *The Masks of God*. In this study, largely but not exclusively, he practices his own form of cultural and mythological yoga, by which I mean to point to the origin of that word, which Campbell obliges by stating: "The Indian term *yoga* is derived from the Sanskrit verbal root *yuj*, 'to link, join, or unite,' which is related etymologically to 'yoke,' a yoke of oxen, and is in sense analogous to the word 'religion' (Latin *re-ligio*), 'to link back, or bind'" (13). I sense that Campbell is perhaps one of the most astute and persistently-practicing scholarly yogis in that his work sustains this quality of "linking back," of sensing analogies where someone else might see only differentiation, separation, even alienation. His work reveals to me the writer's intense desire to burst through "the illusion of duality, [which] is the trick of *maya*. 'Thou art that' (*tat tvam asi*) is the proper thought for the first step to wisdom" (14). By collapsing the *I* of myself into the *Thou* of the other, dualism is usurped, a linkage is established, and a consciousness of wholeness is approached, if not achieved. Herein lies the heartbeat of Campbell's life work as I understand it.

Moreover, something else is roiling about in these early pages of this volume. He wishes at the same time to further "the basic difference between the Oriental and Occidental approaches to the cultivation of the soul" (15), a distinction I wish to link back to throughout this essay. Campbell designs it this way:

> ...spiritual maturity, as understood in the modern Occident, requires a differentiation of *ego* from *id*, whereas in the Orient, throughout the history at least of every teaching that has stemmed from India, ego (*aham-kara*: the making of the sound 'I') is impugned as the principle of libidinous delusion, to be dissolved. (15)

What I wish the reader to note in the above distinction is the place of history in the making of such a constant position derived from India and to hold that for a moment, to be linked to an observation Campbell delineates a few pages later. Ever a storyteller, he deploys narratives themselves to press home an observation or an insight. In relating the story of the "Buddha-to-be," the prince Gautama Shakyamuni, he follows him on his quest wherein the young man "seeks the knowledge that should release all beings from sorrow" (17) until he reaches the still point of the revolving universe, which, Campbell observes, "is described here in mythological terms, lest it should be taken for a physical place to be sought somewhere on earth. For its location is psychological" (17). He continues by affirming that this point is one of balance and equilibrium, and more importantly, it is "in the mind from which the universe can be perfectly regarded: the still-standing point of disengagement around which all things turn" (17). The world as it presents itself is as much a matter of mind as it is mind over matter. Mindfulness grows directly from this recognition.

I find these statements by him in relatively close succession to be marrying several important stems of thought: history, spiritual awakening, mythology and psychology. Blended together in Campbell's life-long studies, these disciplines, together with his passion for wisdom embodied in multiple, but primarily Western, literary traditions, comprise the mythic mystic that is this unique student of world mythologies. In addition, his citation above is cautionary, and one he tirelessly repeated throughout his life: mistaking the vehicle of an image for the tenor of its reality to which it points. This confusion, I sense, occurs when the condition of mind is literal rather than poetically contemplative, as he reminds us in speaking of the image of the Promised Land: "Its connotation—that is, its real meaning—however, is of a spiritual place in the heart that can only be entered by contemplation" (*Thou Art That* 7).

I refer the reader back to Campbell's distinction above that "the supporting point of the universe" within Shakyamuni's quest is described in mythological terms "lest it should be taken for a physical place." Here is a pivot point of contention for Campbell: to mistake, as he will say later, borrowing an old image from Buddhism of the finger pointing at the moon, for the moon itself; in the postmodern lingo of literary criticism, to mistake the signifier for the thing signified. To do so is to commit a cardinal mythological transgression: to take the metaphor literally, or to mistake the symbol for what is now to be understood symbolically, or to take the figure for the ground. A more accurate and engaging interpretation derails at just this juncture of track switching.

The Energy of Myth and Mysticism

When literalism deflects the symbolic order of awareness, the mythic life dissociates and collapses; when it does, the mystical element of awareness, which I believe is the end of Campbell's own pilgrimage towards understanding, evaporates as blue haze. I say this because of another refrain he uses in several of his writings: first, he suggests, is the literal stories that comprise the myth; but if that mythos is alive and vibrant, animated by symbols, then it serves the culture and the individual through "four fundamental functions: the mystical, the cosmological, the sociological and the psychological" *(Pathways* 25). Embedded in all of these functions, it seems to me, is the symbol, which Campbell defines in another context as "an energy-evoking and directing agent. When given a meaning, either corporeal or spiritual, it serves for the engagement of the energy to itself" *(Flight* 143). The mythical therefore, driven by the energies of the symbol, is that point midway between the sensate world and the mystical realm of being, a path on which Campbell as mystic and monk is always tending as the goal of the journey. Artists themselves, he believes, are an essential part of the hero mythos, for they are called, he asserts, "to cast the new images of mythology. That is, they provide the contemporary metaphors that allow us to realize the transcendent, infinite and abundant nature of being as it is" *(Thou Art That* 6). Culturally, we might best look to the artists to restrain us from becoming so overly denotative in our interpretative projects that we lose the connotative ground that artists insist we see as eternal analogies of Being. Figure trumps fact in this universe of imaginal beings, the population and actors of mythical dramas.

He phrases it slightly differently when in conversation with Michael Toms, who interviewed Campbell over a ten year period, beginning in 1975. In this conversation, Campbell recalls another insight from the East: "Another lesson in Buddhism is if you see the Buddha coming down the road, run away. Because if you concretize the divine in any fixed image and say 'There it is' you're off course" *(An Open Life* 66). Toms suggests "We're really talking about the Great Mystery, the ineffable" to which Campbell replies: "That's what we're talking about. It's exciting to talk about it" (66). In their continued discussion the archetype of the Wasteland edges into the conversation. For Campbell it is a powerful and perduring image, in part because it depicts the life of so many people. He pushes the idea of the Wasteland toward the psychological and spiritual condition to which it refers:

> The moment the life process stops, it starts drying up; and the whole sense of myth is finding the courage to follow the process . . . that's what hell is: the place of people who could not yield their ego system to allow the grace of a transpersonal power to move them. (67)

In his own manner and style, the mythologist taps into the source and place of energy that I believe underlies all of his writings: the energy wellspring is the transcendent unknowable to which the powers of metaphor lead one. Kant outlines "a simple formula for the proper reading of a metaphysical symbol" (*The Flight of the Wild Gander* 50). In the four part schema—a is to b as c is to x—what intrigued Campbell is that "x represents a quantity that is not only unknown but absolutely unknowable—which is to say, metaphysical" (51). However, metaphor carries in its vital organs a source of energy that has the capacity to lead one to the ungraspable x. From this point we have the capacity to intuit it, to know it by analogy and figure; it is, however, an indirect knowing which may carry riches that direct knowing fails to provide.

In an Irish context, this very energy has been called *Dana*, named after the Tuatha De Danann, whom Frank MacEowen refers to as ancient "earth-loving people in the Celtic past" who embodied "a tradition beneath the traditions, an undercurrent simmering and churning beneath what is called 'Celtic' or 'Druid' tradition" (*The Spiral of Memory and Belonging* 27).[1] They were a people intimate with the force and energy "of the spiral powers of the earth and spirit" (28). MacEowen's own travels in Ireland attuned him to the "primordial power" that he believes inhabits the swirl of the spiral, a spiralic life force or principle of power.

Now without "going Celtic" in these musings, I do want to insist that there is a correlation and communion between myth, mysticism, mystery and energy, what in another context the British biologist Rupert Sheldrake, whose work was familiar to and quoted by Campbell, calls morphogenetic fields and which the former calls the mythogenetic zone: "And the mythogenetic zone, [is] the primary region of origin of the myths…" (*Flight* 78), wherein energy coagulates and folds back on itself. I suggest that the spiral is the motion of myth in this more precise way: my reading of Campbell aggravates two questions that spiral back on one another: 1. In what ways is myth historical? 2. In what ways is history mythic? Might it be that myth is: the inner sleeve of history?[2] Might history be the informing temporal agent of what is beyond time, space and causality? To press further: how does myth, which explores, discovers and voices the timeless and the transcendent, or at the very least, lead a soul to this space?

He outlines the first function of myth in the face of affirming, negating or reforming the world as it is, as that force that arouses "in the mind a sense of awe before this situation through one of three ways of participating in it" (*Thou* 3); for my purposes in this essay, the first function is most essential, for Campbell regards it "as the essentially religious function of mythology—that is, the mystical function" by which the individual comes into direct contact "with the mystery of being" (3).

In her simple but powerful abridged version of a more staggering study of Mysticism, Evelyn Underhill writes of the ordinary man of common sense: he orders and arranges his world to "reducible little squares" (*Practical Mysticism* 19) which are static and safe elements to guide his sense of the real. But on the other side, she affirms that the neat and orderly patterns of the woven work "are short ends, clumsy joins and patches; all of these disturb my simple philosophy" (19). Behind the manicured hedges of my ordered world of appearances, where I would place the historical self's reality, is another, more confusing and very differently-organized landscape of myth. The mythical and the mystical are both in the fabric of reality, but backside. This backside of things is the realm of Campbell's exploration and the texture of his design as mystically-situated explorer of the inherent mystery embroidered in all that is.

"To give up one's own comfortably upholstered universe" is the task of the artist, the poet and the mystic, Underhill further affirms, that places one closer to the animals, in that like animals, "the mystic and the poet strive for a directness of apprehension which we have lost. The terrier gets and responds to the real smell, not a notion or a name" (27). That "real smell" one arrives at through the imaginal act of contemplation Underhill describes as "the essential activity of all artists," one which embodies "a virginal outlook on all things, a celestial power of communion with veritable life, when sensation is freed from the tyranny of thought" (28). Perhaps, to push the analogy one more waltzing step, W.B. Yeats writes, in one of the most formidable works on "Ireland's mystical and spiritual tradition," *Mythologies*, that before he can be initiated into the tradition of alchemy, he must learn the complex steps of "a magical dance, *for rhythm was the wheel of Eternity*, on which alone the transient and accidental could be broken, and the spirit set free" (286, my italics). The mystic, the poet and the animal participate in this eternal round of the rhythm of life itself. My offering is that Joseph Campbell, in his own bodily vitality, his love of and player of music, his gourmet appetite, his love of the geishas, participated in such an elegant and exuberant energy flow of the universe.

Now there are dozens of definitions and descriptions of the mystic. I am suggesting here, however, that what unites in the soul of Joseph Campbell are the complementary impulses of mythologist, poet, mystic and historian, wrapped in the psychological gauze or gossamer of depth psychology as outlined and promoted by C.G. Jung. Recursivity, coil and recoil, spiraling, retrieval, deepening, a love of metaphor and its necessity, the folding back of energy and patterns of consciousness both individually and collectively—all these are skeins working in bits and "joins" on the backside of Campbell's intricately woven and braided prose studies of myth.

Journeying and Journaling into Destiny

I base the above proposition in part on two of his works that, to date, have not been widely read or discussed, but which make up the qualitative backdrop of his inflections towards the mystical. Both *Baksheesh and Brahman* as well as *Sake and Satori* are the extended and often neatly polished journals of Campbell he kept during his year-long pilgrimage around the world in 1954-55 at the age of 50. In that journey, a spiraling of sorts around the globe, he not only discovered and settled on his life work; he also came to inhabit a certain *habitus* of mind, an exuberance of body and a *gravitas* of spirit that molted into the mystic he became through a favorite pastime of his: brooding. He writes for instance on Wednesday, September 8, 1954 in Amarnath, India as he travels to a temple by car with friends: "During the drive I had time to brood a bit more on the Indian problem" *(Baksheesh* 22).

One reads in these early journal entries the growth and further sophistication of an analogical imagination, one which discerns relationship, connectedness and commonality through the clear sharp eyes of differentiation; he learns to envision a Oneness foraging amongst the Many. Multiplicity in India breeds in Campbell a vision of an underlying Unity, a pattern of exploration that he would continue to sharpen for the rest of his days. Two pages, 22-23, are illustrations of his thought processes, his listings—he adored lists and used them everywhere as compressed ordering principles!—as a way of seeing in history, in memory, patterns of mythic presences. And then, in a slight lifting of the veil that accompanies one of Campbell's fictional heroes, Stephen Daedelus, as he walks the strand in Joyce's *A Portrait of the Artist as a Young Man,* and suffers in one unplanned knee-buckling instant what Joyce referred to as "esthetic arrest," Campbell offers this poetic, even lyric, description of an analogous emotional moment:

> Last evening, during our boat ride, I saw a woman standing alone, in one of those canal-vistas, and she seemed to me to be linked to nature in the way of these people, that is to say, linked to nature by being linked to a principle beyond nature, through a ritual attitude, something very different from the romantic return to nature and intuition of God through nature. *(Baksheesh* 22-23)

Being related both *to* and *beyond* at the same instant is the everlasting thump of mystical experience and Campbell's participation in it. These two italicized prepositions are, as well, mythic propositions of one connected to and transcendent of the material world. For Campbell, a mystical sense is: 1. esthetic; 2. mythic; 3. historical; 4. poetic; 5. depth psychological. In his fine chapter on Joyce's *A Portrait of the Artist,* Campbell draws a dramatic comparison between Dante's beholding Beatrice Portinari in the streets of 14th century Florence and Stephen's coming upon the woman on the strand that sparks or ignites an instant of "esthetic arrest" (19). "It is an eternal moment…. What he sees is not simply a lovely girl, but a ray of light of eternity. It opens his third eye (his inward eye); the world drops back a dimension; his life is now committed to this seizure" (*Mythic Worlds* 19). Stephen's version of bliss is carved out for him in this crux, or crossroad, of time and eternity made possible and poignant by the intrusion of beauty into the querulous quotidian. Esthetics, mimesis, myth and the mystical congeal in his imagination in an instant. My thesis is that just such a sensibility was also Campbell's guiding shaman in his mature work, which gave a decidedly mystical cast to his thought and writing.

However, one more ingredient is necessary at such a rich juncture of mystery and matter: the *sublime*. Continuing with the image and nature of beauty that Joyce outlines in the spirit of Thomistic theory in *Portrait,* Campbell rests on the quality of radiance that accompanies esthetic arrest: "If it's a radiance that doesn't overwhelm you, we call it beauty. But if the radiance so diminishes your ego that you are in an almost transcendent rapture, this is the sublime. What renders the sublime is immense space or immense power." What such a moment of transcendence that expands immediately and forcefully one's orbit of awareness leads to is "a beautiful accord" . . . the "enchantment of the heart" (23). Discovery, recognition, rapture, release, rejoicing—the properties of such an encounter in and through the material world is an experience that preoccupied Campbell as he searched with abandon through world mythologies for this moment in human consciousness.

Such an experience of the sublime, moreover, is not alien to another of Campbell's trenchant interests: history itself in its relation to myth. We gain an inkling of such import for him in the philosopher Schopenhauer's insight into the unfolding of a human life. His essay, "An Apparent Intention in the Fate of the Individual," outlines how so many people and events we encounter in the pilgrimage of our lives seem gratuitous, accidental, haphazard as we live through them: "Then you get on in your sixties or seventies and look back, your life looks like a well-planned novel with a coherent theme. Things have happened, you realize, in an appropriate way" (*Mythic Worlds* 286). Structure and coherence replace the chance quality of those events seen from an angle of the present; now, recollected in a backward gaze, one sees pattern, accord, coherence, theme, congruence, relevance where before there was a chaotic array of incidents and characters with no interior design.

I would push Campbell's idea of a novel taking shape in one's life here into a little lower layer. What one discovers is the mytho-poetic character of one's being in its temporal becoming, arrangement, order and coherence; and contrary to Schopenhauer's question: Who wrote all of these? Which answer is: "You did" (286), I would entertain the possibility of more hands at the writing desk of one's life than one's own inscribing self. In addition, Campbell's example from Schopenhauer suggests some further reveries on one's personal memories, a larger mythic pattern embracing it, and a discovery of the unique—ok, novel—mythos that one has been spinning out of herself. Memory, history, mythos and an awareness of some patterning accord between them is as well another corridor of the mystical sense that Campbell's work engages. I assert this last point because I believe it underlines another of his observations expressed earlier in the same volume in a discussion with an audience after he has lectured on Joyce's fiction.

Campbell returns to one of his most heat-generating themes: the nature of God: "God isn't a fact. God is a symbol. As soon as you interpret God as a fact, you are off the beam.... As I have said, deities in mythological systems are personifications of energies" (275). And then just below, he continues: But where I have used the word *God*, let us simply say *Brahman*, a neuter noun that refers past itself to the mystery of the total energy of life" (275). His focus on energy is bedrock to his theory and function of the hero outlined so fully in *The Hero with a Thousand Faces* that brought mythic discourse back into high fashion. That is, the hero appears at those moments of crisis in culture when the energy flow between the macrocosm and the microcosm has ceased movement.

The hero's task, which s/he must first hear, then heed by giving up self for a higher achievement, is to restore the flow of the life energy between the cosmos and the collective as well as individual psyche. He observes early in the study: "for the hero as the incarnation of God is himself the navel of the world, the umbilical point through which the energies of eternity break into time" (49). A successful, if you will, heroic quest is, as Campbell asserts, "the unlocking and release again of the flow of life into the body of the world. The miracle of this flow may be represented in physical terms as a circulation of food substance, dynamically as a streaming of energy, or spiritually as a manifestation of grace" (40).

My own reading here is that the energy field or principle is the goal and source of all understanding of mythic thought and sense. I believe it worthy to notice as well that the hero is not *in relation to* God but shares that same *identity as* God. The terms of relation and identity is another staple Campbell motif in his writings; to be incarnated as God elevates the soul of the hero and the heroic potential that resides, most often sleeping in a coiled state, but surfacing in one's dream life, within every individual. In addition, these essential energy fields reveal the deepest patterns in human life and were discerned by Campbell, in important moments, during his year-long pilgrimage in 1954-55, to which I now wish to return.

Distance and Discernment

Before we leave India with Campbell and travel to southeast Asia, we should pause for a moment to listen to how this trip released in him a full grasp of his life's work. Much akin to James Joyce, who chose finally to exit Ireland in order to write about her, so did Campbell feel a necessity to leave his normal life and work in order to discern in what direction it needed to develop. Early on in his Indian sojourn, he comes to this recognition:

> What I am to study is definitely here: folk religion, with its roots in the deep past; aristocratic religion, represented in the ruins of the temple art of India; the phenomenon of the sadhu—past, present, future.... Moreover, it is just possible that there maybe someone in all of this from whom I may wish to learn something fundamental. (*Baksheesh* 23)

His experiences in India develop two complementary impulses in him: one is the power of the human spirit amongst oppressive poverty to remain serene, content and spiritually rich; the second is the increasing value of Western consciousness that he thirsts to step back into with greater enthusiasm: "The hope, the immediate teacher of the modern world is the West. The main problems of the modern world are functions of the Western style of life and thought. The most significant approach to the modern problems, therefore, must be via the modern Western psyche—and most emphatically, via the modern American psyche" (165). His expression here is prologue to a profound awakening in his life's trajectory, delineated in the following manner: "This realization has moved me to dissolve my earlier thoughts of a series of works on Oriental religion and legend…and to plan to concentrate on the legendary mythological themes of the West— . . ." (*Baksheesh* 165).

Later, and closer to his time of returning to America, Campbell in Kyoto, Japan suffers both a disillusionment with his proposed long-term projects as well as incisive clarity about his life's professional design. Startled by an essay he reads in *Time* on 9 May 1955 by C.S. Lewis in an inaugural lecture as Medieval Studies scholar delivered at Cambridge, Campbell is stunned by Lewis' announcing "a new archetypal image" into history: that of old machines "being superceded by new and better ones" *(Sake* 102). This replacement addresses a larger archetype, which seems the real emphasis of Lewis' address, namely, the impulse to constantly attain new goods and provisions rather than conserve what we have as "'the cardinal business of life, would most shock and bewilder [our ancestors].… I conclude that it is the greatest change in the history of Western man…'" (qtd. in *Sake* 102). Acquisition and consumption are the new archetypal patterns of being that, Lewis asserts, will and may have already replaced conserving and sustaining as patterns of behavior in the West.

His insights pulls Campbell up short to evaluate his own projects. Here he draws a parallel with Buddhism's idea that "'All is without a self' would seem to me to go along very well with the idea of the discarded machines (though not, indeed, with that of striving for goods we have never yet had)" (102). He descends into disillusionment with the Oriental way of thought and life, it seems to me, preferring instead to retrench his future work in historical and philological scholarship—"let's not then try to read our own reactions back into Oriental context" (103). Lewis' making evident a new archetypal pattern emerging in the West persuades Campbell to shy away from his earlier epic plan: "All of this implies great warnings and danger signals for me in the work ahead on my *Basic Mythologies of Mankind*" (103), works that will eventually materialize into the multivolume *The Masks of God.*

In addition, his shifting mythology is accompanied by a reassessed methodology in typical Campbell fashion, a series of items drawn up in a crisp, succinct list:

1. Beginning from the beginning, I am to follow motifs objectively and historically. Also, I am to record interpretations objectively and historically, on the basis of contemporary texts. (*Sake* 103)

The list is too involved to duplicate here, except for this final item in it which is a colossal shift in the way Campbell would conduct his studies, now that he has absorbed experientially the worlds of India, Southeast Asia and Japan. My own belief is that without this year-long journey he would not have arrived at what follows, or at least not so early as he did to pursue it with success and which is finally orchestrated by Bill Moyers and him in *The Power of Myth,* the most ubiquitous of all he wrote and created for television: "3. The historical milestone represented is that of the recognition of the actual unity of human culture (the diffusion and parallelism of myths).... The time has come for a global, rather than provincial, history of the images of thought" (*Sake* 103). These words comprise his big picture, his grand design and his epic vision. He ends his list with a promise to adhere to the little picture: "5. Make no great cross-cultural leaps, and even within a given culture, do not try to harmonize what philosophers of that culture itself have not harmonized. Stick to the historical perspectives and all will emerge of itself" (*Sake* 103). Already familiar with and highly influenced by Oswald Spengler's *Decline of the West* when he wrote *Hero,* Campbell seems to be aligning himself in a moment of great resolve with Spengler's sense of history, who himself wrote of "the metaphysically exhausted soil of the West" (*Decline* 5). What Spengler proposed and Campbell assumes the mantel of, is a morphological grasp of history in which one discovers "from a morphological angle, disparate events will take on under examination 'deep uniformities'" (*Decline* 6). The symbol and the archetype are for Spengler categories of understanding so that "the whole of mythological religions and artistic thought . . . constitutes the essence and kernel of all history" (7). Spengler assists Campbell in blending the disciplines of psychology, religion, mythology and artistic expressions into a palimpsest and a palette from which he will paint for himself a new inflection of the mythopoetic imagination given fullest commerce in History. [3]

History and Psychic Energy

I wish to devote the last pages of this article to Campbell's sustained interest in psychic and spiritual energy that flows from earth, individual, culture, outward to the wider cosmos and back again, as a spiralic loop that world mythologies give voice to in ritual, rites of passage, narratives and other forms of incarnate expression. Not to be overlooked or reduced here as well is Campbell's own explorations and love of the smallest forms of life, the seedling and budding plant given elegant display in volume II, Part 2: *The Way of the Seeded Earth* comprising a section of *The Historical Atlas of World Mythology*, his love and study of *The Way of the Animal Powers*, as well as his decades-long colloquy with body worker, Stanley Keleman in *Myth and the Body*. I showcase these works especially at this point because, as a mystic engaged in the transcendent oneness of creation, Campbell is, as many mystical expressions confirm, deeply rooted in the material imagination, the seedlings, as it were, of a full mystical fructification.

I have written elsewhere that "psychic and spiritual energy, though not divorced from matter but actually inhering within it, within Mother Earth, seems to be one of Campbell's perennial and abiding concerns" ("What's Up History's Inner Sleeve: Myth and the Fabric of Culture" 1). My sense is that the principle of energy as a life force derived both from his study of world mythologies as well as his abiding study of C.G. Jung's work, especially, I suspect, Jung's powerful essay, "On Psychic Energy," a centerpiece of his *Structure and Dynamics of the Psyche* (¶s1-130). Yet this energy is materially-inflected, ubiquitous and links spirit, psyche and cosmos. Consider his early insight in *Animal Powers*: poets and artists today are present in large measure

> to perform the work of the first and second functions of a
> mythology by recognizing through the veil of nature . . . the

radiance, terrible yet gentle, or the dark, unspeakable light beyond, and through their words and images to reveal the sense of the vast silence that is the ground of us all and of all beings. (10)

Campbell refers here to the first function of a mythology: "to awaken and maintain in the individual a sense of wonder and participation in the mystery of this finally inscrutable universe" (8); the second "is to fill every particle and quarter of the current cosmological image with its measure of this mystical import" (8). Myths, therefore, are both current to a culture or a people as well as provide a current of energy flow through the grounded gravity of silence, itself an energy field embodied in image.

Furthermore, the body for Campbell is no small player in this cosmic drama of mythic sustenance. He reminds us, for instance, in *The Flight of the Wild Gander* that "myths are the texts of the rites of passage" (34) having their origins in the energies of the organs of the body, both in conflict and in complement to one another. He furthers this idea in *The Power of Myth*: "the archetypes of the unconscious are manifestations of the organs of the body and their powers. Archetypes are biologically grounded..." (51). Musing on this same idea in another context, I wrote:

> A renewed or revisioned mythos might then include an ability to reimagine the relation of spirit, body and earth in a constant but benevolent dialogic tension between the body's interiority and the world's matter, mediated by the social customs that comprise a specific historical time and place. ("The Myth of Nature and the Nature of Myth" 31)

To leap another step forward in pursuing this energy trail that snakes through his writings, especially the later ones, in *The Inner Reaches of Outer Space* Campbell observes that "the energy by which the body is pervaded is the same as that which illuminates the world and maintains alive all being, the two breaths being the same" (41).

Such a unitary vision of a comprehensive design of the world's interior and exterior natures he inherited, at least in seedling form, from Ananda K. Coomaraswamy, who Campbell observes of his thought: he "could maintain that the metaphysical principles symbolized in India in the dreamlike imagery of myth are implicit in mythology everywhere" (34) and goes on to quote from Coomaraswamy's own writing, in which he affirms "an underlying spiritual unity of the human race" (34): "'...the various cultures of mankind are no more than the dialects of one and the same spiritual language'" (*Flight* 34).

I have not attempted nor wanted to put sack cloth and ashes or even a crisp Cistercian garment on Joseph Campbell and attire him in what he is not. However, this contemplative extrovert returns repeatedly to the grand synthesis or design of a world *monomyth*, a term he inherited from James Joyce, that attends and informs his exploration of myth with a decidedly spiritual cast and one which highlights Jung's inspiration of the *unus mundus*. Furthermore, there exists in his prose a coiled, or if I may return to the spiral image here as I bring this brief excursus to completion, energy structure: it folds back, remembers itself, loops back through history and sees by way of analogy the power of myth's presence in the world psyche. Campbell continually intuits a secret harmony between the human being embodied and, as he writes, forms of the macrocosm that are given voice and substance by the miraculous imaginal power of metaphor, what he affirmed repeatedly as "the native tongue of myth" (*Thou Art That* 45).

Images of mythology are all metaphorical of a reality that can only be intuited, never known. Campbell suggests further in the work that I believe most deeply grooves the prominence of metaphor: that the universe might best be imagined as "a living being in the image of a great mother, within whose womb all the worlds, both of life and death, had their existence." Analogy, or an analogical imagination, rests squarely here: "the human body is a duplicate, in miniature, of that macrocosmic form. Throughout the whole a secret harmony holds sway. It is the function of mythology and relevant rites to make this macro-microcosmic insight known to us..." (45).

The images of myth are metaphors, symbolic at the same time of vital energies that traverse the cosmos through and into the individual, through the mesocosm of particular and specific cultural and tribal customs. A deep and thick relationship attends such an energy flow, or even energy transfer system, wherein mythic images carry both intellectual, historical and affective powers to guide the psyche as they direct psychic energy. That Campbell intuited, then traced these divine powers of presence and their capacity to ignite in ritual remembrance, is a sign of his monkish and mystically inflected imagination.

In a discussion on "Earthrise: The Dawning of a New Spiritual Awareness" appended to *Thou Art That*, he sounds the final note, for this exploration anyway, about myth's elaborate design: "Myth has many functions. The first we might term mystical, in that myth makes a connection between our waking consciousness and the whole mystery of the universe. That is its cosmological function..." (103).

Let's leave him there, beaming, in fine company, nested deep in dialogue, as if he were in an Irish pub in Kinvara, Killarney or Dublin, thinking once more about the place of the imagination in mythic pilgrimaging. An engaging icon for the extraverted soul, Campbell was also a devout solitary: brooding over his studies, musing over his spiraling sentences that often go on for the better part of a hefty paragraph with seemingly inexhaustible rhetorical vitality, he never tired of thinking through myth to the mystical. His energy transported him to the image of the Earthrise, a spectacular photo taken from the moon. That image, he pondered, is the great cosmic bumper sticker to usher in a new mythos, where so many of the borderlines drawn by human fear and fatigue are suddenly liquefied, leaving only the blurred edges of oceans and land, clouds and wind patterns, and a human imagination to revel at their mysterious design, their sacred narrative, their trenchant moment in a cosmic story, still unfolding, still enfolding and willing to embrace us all.

Endnotes

[1] Another image to explore in relation to the Celtic spiral is that of the coiled Kundalini serpent depicted with such majesty in *The Inner Reaches* (56) which as symbol of "an original knowledge" in its 3.5 spiralic turns suggests a primordial disposition of psyche.

[2] "What's Up History's Inner Sleeve? Myth and the Fabric of Culture." Presented at a symposium entitled *Myth, Memory and Culture,* jointly sponsored by The Dallas Institute of Humanities and Culture under the direction of Dr. J. Larry Allums, and Pacifica Graduate Institute, May 11-12, 2007 in Dallas, Texas.

[3] Of course I am bypassing the other earlier pilgrimage Campbell

inaugurated during the years 1927-28, as Richard Tarnas writes, "to study in Paris and Munich, where he first encountered the work of Freud, Jung, Joyce, Mann and Picasso and conceived his understanding of the mythic foundations of human experience" (*Cosmos and Psyche* 331). Nor am I developing the cosmic conjunctions that Tarnas' magisterial study of cosmos' influence on psyche in history develops so eloquently and thoroughly.

Works Cited

Bodkin, Maud. *Archetypal Patterns in Poetry: Psychological Studies of Imagination.* London: Oxford UP, 1965.

Campbell, Joseph. *A Skeleton Key to Finnegans Wake: Unlocking James Joyce's Masterwork.* Ed. Edmund L. Epstein. Novato, California: New World Library, 2005.

---. *Baksheesh and Brahman: Asian Journals—India.* Ed. Robin and Stephen Larsen. Novato, California: New World Library, 1995.

---. *Mythic Worlds, Modern Words: Joseph Campbell on the Art of James Joyce.* Ed. Edmund L. Epstein. Novato, California: New World Library, 2003.

---. *Pathways to Bliss: Mythology and Personal Transformation.* Novato, California: New World Library, 2004.

---. *Sake and Satori: Asian Journals—Japan.* Ed. David Kudler. Novato, California: New World Library, 2002.

---. *The Flight of the Wild Gander: Explorations in the Mythological Dimension.* Novato, California: New World Library, 2001.

---. *The Hero With a Thousand Faces.* Bollingen Series XVII. Princeton: Princeton UP, 1973.

---. *The Inner Reaches of Outer Space: Metaphor as Myth and as Religion.* Novato, California: New World Library, 2003.

---. *The Power of Myth.* Ed. Betty Sue Flowers. New York: Doubleday, 1988.

---. *The Way of the Animal Powers.* Vol. 1. *Historical Atlas of World Mythology.* Alfred Van Der Marck Editions. London: Summerfield P, 1983.

---. *The Way of the Seeded Earth.* Vol. 2. Part 2: *Mythologies of the Primitive Planters: The Northern Americans. Historical Atlas of World Mythology.* New York: Harper and Row, nd.

---. *Thou Art That: Transforming Religious Metaphor.* Ed. Eugene

Kennedy. Novato, California: New World Library, 2001.

---. *The Masks of God: Oriental Mythology*. New York: Viking P, 1962.

Jung, C.G. "On Psychic Energy." *The Structure and Dynamics of the Psyche*. Trans. R.F.C. Hull. Vol. 8. Bollingen Series XX. New York: Pantheon Books, 1960. 3-66.

Keleman, Stanley. *Myth and the Body. A Colloquy with Joseph Campbell*. Berkeley: Center P, 1999.

Larsen, Stephen and Robin Larsen. *Joseph Campbell: A Fire in the Mind. The Authorized Biography*. Rochester, VT: Inner Traditions, 2002.

MacEowen, Frank. *The Spiral of Memory and Belonging: A Celtic Path of Soul and Kinship*. Novato, California: New World Library, 2004.

Slattery, Dennis Patrick. "The Myth of Nature and the Nature of Myth: Becoming Transparent to Transcendence." *The International Journal of Transpersonal Studies,* 2005, vol. 24. 29-38. Reprinted in *Harvesting Darkness: Essays on Literature, Myth, Film and Culture*. New York: iUniverse, 2006. 288-310.

---. "What's Up History's Inner Sleeve? Myth and the Fabric of Culture." Presented at a conference: "Myth, Memory and Culture," at The Dallas Institute of Humanities and Culture, Dallas, Texas. May 11-12, 2007.

Spengler, Oswald. "Form and Actuality." Vol. One. *The Decline of the West*. Trans. Charles Francis Atkinson. New York: Knopf, 1948.

Tarnas, Richard. *Cosmos and Psyche: Intimations of a New World Order*. New York: Viking P, 2006.

Toms, Michael. *An Open Life: Joseph Campbell in Conversation with Michael Toms*. Ed. John M. Maher and Dennie Briggs. Burdet, New York: Larson Publications, 1988.

Underhill, Evelyn: *Practical Mysticism and Abba*. New York: Dutton, 1914.

Yeats, William Butler. *Mythologies*. New York: Touchstone Books, Simon and Schuster, 1998.

CHAPTER 5

VIOLENT DESIGNS:
IMAGINING VIOLENCE AS PHYSICAL
AND FICTIONAL

A wound does not have to be described
in order to be felt.
~Amin Maalouf, *In the Name of Identity:*
Violence and the Need to Belong 6

The intention of this essay is to remain faithful to three different experiences of violence in order to discern what lies within the folds of this most enigmatic and contradictory of human impulses. It will therefore consist of three "moments," if you will, of violence.

I. *We Must Warn You: Some of These Scenes May Be Disturbing*

Let's begin with a personal experience of violence. Some time ago I was driving to the grocery store in Carpinteria, California. I pulled left in front of a slow moving car to park in the lot. From the other driver's point of view, I had cut him off, invaded his space, upset his life and he wanted revenge to balance the scales that had not only suffered disequilibrium but had been downright unhinged. He squealed his tires and pulled in behind me, blocking me from any hasty and untimely escape until he could have his way with me.

I exited my car and turned towards the heat of a red face squirting obscenities with the alacrity of a bull snorting down the streets of Pamplona. Boy was this guy pissed! Before I could focus on what was happening, he spit in my face and began swinging. Now normally I am pretty good about taking care of myself, but this guy was BIG and frothy and mad. In my Irish knee jerk response, and beyond all categories of reason, I spit back in his face with the little saliva I could muster, and began swinging back, more to defend then to debilitate or disable. He loomed over me with the heat of Mars, the rage of millennia and the reasoning of a gnat. I had it all in one smoky package. Fight or flight were hot contenders in the boxing ring of my diminished reasoning in the instant.

Cursing and swearing about my driving acumen, he took a step back when I swung with some authority at his bullying ways. I took off my glasses for fear that broken glass in my eye would not serve me well the next time I tried to read a passage from Dante's *Inferno*— for here I was looking into its fiery abandon at a soul who had never heard of Dante, much less of Beatrice or any signals of due measure. I was, in short, on my own, dizzy from the attack, yet cerebral enough to realize that if I provoke this behemoth by some derogatory wise crack about his mother and the conditions of his origins, I was lentil soup in a broken ladle. His stream of curses continued as he moved back towards his car, secure in the notion that he had successfully scared the shit out of me. I'll sign that affidavit after my hand stops quaking.

I wanted to comment on what a stooge he looked like with a hat slightly ajar from his assault on me, but restrained, having grown fond of the teeth in my head and a strong wish to have them stay in their current positions. This violent assault was over in a few moments. But not really. In fact, it had hardly begun. I looked around to a small crowd that had gathered for the free freak show unfolding in front of them. I was indeed on display.

He drove off, tires still smoking as signal to his setting things right. I was disheveled, confused, unmoored from my shopping list and, well, not even hungry. And then I was angry that I had not attacked him with more gusto, even though I knew that the consequences of such silliness could have put me in the hospital, perhaps long enough to miss this conference[1] and my impending classes. One has to make choices. I slowed down, or tried to. I was proud that I did not back down to this bully's advances, but I was demoralized from the attack. I smelled the sputum on my face and became nauseous. I skipped shopping for food; the incentive was way past gone. I drove home and showered. Yes, showered to get the sickening smell of his saliva and the sound of his curses off me; somehow they too clung to my clothing. And more: the left side of my face hurt, stung really, from where he must have caught me. I felt nothing in the moment, a sting of shame in the wake of it all. Adrenaline, my guess was, had numbed me like Novocain before the drill. But now, like a stinging memory, my face registered the reality of the fight and its enraged aftermath. My teeth had, however, been up to the attack; they were, in a word, unbroken.

I suppose in all fairness I should also report that my lower back, hurting for four days because of pulling it early in the morning as I stooped to pick up a suitcase, no longer hurt—this lug had cured it by creating such a flight/fight response in me that the adrenaline erased the pain. I felt both hurt and healed. But something else began to worm its way into my consciousness: exhilaration, even a form of ecstasy over the battle, not won, certainly, but survived without backing down, all teeth and bones in their proper alignment. The violence was, as one might say, a RUSH. I don't recommend cutting people off or trolling the highways looking for impatient Cretins to do battle with in order to jump start some excitement in your life; but I realized that the short and mercifully little damaging altercation had altered my state of being. The violence had both unnerved and energized me. Violence had shoved me into another level of consciousness, of seeing and feeling differently. Fighting back such a formidable foe had revved consciousness to a level I had not experienced in some time. I felt alive and full of vitality. Ares on the half-shell.

Was it the violence itself as an experience that both threatened my well being as well as enlivened my soul to the degree that, while I did not want to find this guy again out there on the asphalt desert, I

71

knew that some connection with a higher, more ecstatic reality had occurred? What was the draw of violence, or at least this form of it? What did it engage? What in the imagination was so responsive and receptive to its presence that violence, I considered for a moment, could be addictive? Violence addicts? Through a direct frontal assault with a violent imagination, I began in the glow of its aftermath, to reflect on the imagination of violence. I had heard of, but never before experienced, the high of combat that military personnel had witnessed. Now I had an inkling of what they were feeling.

In the leeward side of such a terrible yet quickening moment, I could think of nothing else but this incident. It bullied and elbowed out of my consciousness any other ideas, images, anticipations as irrelevant, so pervasive did its ooze coat my mind and behavior for several days. This impatient fellow, a bully who short-circuited any reasoned response with the more quick-fix of violence, forced me to reflect on the difference between a soul possessed of a violent imagination and an imagination of violence.

Let me offer a few reflections on what I wrote about in my journal the next two mornings, a kind of linguistic or rhetorical version of showering after such an invasion—a *katharsis* or ritual purging or cleansing of sorts that I find writing allows for and often even insists on. I will confess at the outset that violence wears so many faces, shows so many realities in its arsenal, can spit in such multiple directions at once, that what I say below applies to this incidence of violence and does not pretend to universalize one or another pedigree:

- Violence is beyond the normative: it approaches or opens up what I would call the landscape of the super-natural, the numinous, and the other-worldly.
- Violence can move us beyond language to what is inexpressible, what will not be tamed by the whip of words.
- Violence alters time. Time stops or disappears altogether. History evaporates.
- Violence alters space, shrinks it, condenses it so that the only space in one's perceptual field is the other.
- Memory is assassinated, later to be resuscitated as the trauma of violence scatters into separate parts.
- A larger frame of reference is destroyed, so all-consuming is

the moment of confrontation with the other, with the desire to inflict harm accompanied by a concomitant terror of being pummeled and injured or killed. One thinks of little else.

- Violence unleashes layers of emotion that are gnarled and knotted together in the event, but begin to separate out and haunt one with uncanny fierceness in their remembrance.
- Violence is a worldview that consumes the entire being of a person, a community, a nation, or a people. Thus, violence appropriates one's ontology, swallows it with an appetite that is unforgiving and insatiable.
- Violence is a primal and predatory worldview, a way of perceiving.
- Violence is a form of imagination, twisted, distorted and without measure. Violence turns boundaries or order into dead meat.
- Violence is a methodology, if not a mythology, for it possesses a manner of making the world present in a new and energetic as well as debilitating way.
- Violence has the capacity to renew and to consume.
- Violence can be hurtful, harmful, as well as healing.
- Violence, up close and personal, can draw quickly to the surface, like the blood that begins to sense an opening around the wound of a knife or a bullet, many of the shadows roiling deeper in the psyche, aspects of one's self that normally purr quietly in the underground of one's being to sustain identity.
- Violence, as a bundled knot of energy, wounds the soul; like a canker it invades, infests, infects, inflects, infiltrates and informs the more reasoned and civil aspects of our being.
- As rape is a form of violence, violence itself in most any packaged reality, is a form of rape. Violence rapes one of something crucial to his/her identity. Violence can steal these same qualities from a nation or an entire people. No wonder that violence against others is often accompanied by raping members of the opposition.

From these reflections, a series of questions began to cut me off, pull up behind me to block and then engage my consciousness of violence:

1. What is violence in the service of?

2. What is it that serves violence?
3. What are its instruments in the individual, the culture, an entire civilization?
4. Is nature violent by design?
5. What does violence wish me to hear, demand that I attend to, that I have perhaps grown deaf to?
6. What does violence want me to see that I have grown blind to?
7. What does violence want me to touch and feel that I have grown numb to?
8. What does a violent act leveled at one do to one's sense of identity?
9. What occurs to a violent act when it is finally small enough to enter in bits and pieces, into memory, there to be transformed?

I ask you to keep one or two of these questions in mind, and of course add to them, as you hear the second part of this story.

2. *If the Shoe Fits: The Voice of Violence*

For years when I taught Rhetoric at Southern Methodist University in Dallas, I asked each freshman student to make one formal presentation to the class as a way of demonstrating some persuasive elements of public speaking. Over 8 years I heard hundreds of presentations, but one in particular, delivered by a young woman, I have never forgotten. This essay is an appropriate place to remember her performance as well as the artistry behind her presentation.

When I called her name, she walked up to the front of the classroom and set her essay on the wooden podium that sat on the top of my desk. Just before beginning, however, she took off one of her dress shoes and set it beside her, with no explanation. We thought it curious, a good luck charm, or a superstition known only to her; however, we turned our attention instead to her beginning. She began by relating a particular shopping trip to the supermarket near campus. Without missing a beat in her reading, she reached over and took the shoe in her hand and slammed the podium with it with such force that we all grimaced, confused. Were we to laugh? Be still? React in some way? We sat in our own bewilderment and continued to listen. We were now ALL ears.

She told of watching a mother shopping with her young son, about 6, who had been asking for some candy in a basket at the head of an aisle. SLAM went the shoe once more on to the podium. The mother, she read, was growing increasingly impatient with her child and told him to shut up or she would put him out in the car to sit by himself until she finished shopping. SLAM went the shoe on the podium. The young boy would not stop pleading with her for at least one piece of candy and the mother, equally adamant, began shouting at him with more energy, and obviously completely indifferent to who was beginning to watch and listen to her berate her son. SLAM went the shoe.

Frustrated by his whining and realizing that her scolding him to be still was not working, the mother drew up her leg and took off one of her shoes. SLAM went the shoe on the podium. Now no one in the room was chuckling. The classroom grew very quiet, except for the voice of the student and the repetitive SLAMS of her shoe. A growing awareness settled on each of us of what the slamming shoe stood for and indeed, remembered. The mother took her shoe by the heel and began to hit the six year old on the top of his head, with no reserve. SLAM went the shoe in the classroom; SLAM went the mother's shoe on the head of her son. We had all grown increasingly uncomfortable and even agitated as the meaning of the slamming shoe descended on each of us in the audience; we heard one story punctuated by a physical witness as we comprehended the student's shoe was that of the mother in the store striking her child because of his relentless desire for a treat.

Now, we were imagining violence along with the student's memory of it; here, the vessel was able to contain the violence in a narrative witnessed firsthand by the speaker. Our imaginations moved over and under and around the story—the narrative of violence had become a violent narrative. We could feel the shoe, in our imaginations, strike the young boy into silence. As the shoe continued to come down on the podium, the slam of understanding spread like a bad bruise in our consciousness. We all began to shift and change under the assault of this dramatic, now grown mimetic, reenactment of what the speaker had witnessed and now struggled, quite successfully, by all accounts, to represent this action through a dramatic reenactment, which now gathered meaning for us sitting more and more quietly in the room.

Well into the talk, we in the audience began to wince when we saw the student raise the shoe over the podium, for now our imaginations were attuned to the child's vulnerable head receiving the blows from his mother. No longer was the student's shoe hitting wood; it had instead metamorphosed poetically into the grotesque solution of a mother meting out violence to a child whose appetite had exceeded his ability to contain it. So too had hers. The mother's own absence of containment met the child's in a clash that allowed one to powerfully subdue the other's desires, but at what cost? Before, where only something monstrous was able to loom into the room, now, in a ripening of understanding, something more humane grew up to add to the poignancy of the event recollected, remembered, related and reflected upon by all of us.

We were transformed by this dramatic witness to violence; outrage, the first installment on our feelings, soon gave way to compassion for the mother whose desperation knew no limits or boundaries—the stuff of tragedy, the tragic impasse of NO EXIT.

The student reading then read: "I could not stand by and watch this. I stepped forward and grabbed the mother's arm in mid-air, at which time she became enraged and tried to bring the shoe down on me. I resisted and struggled with her; just then the store manager intervened and pulled the woman from me and the child away from her. He called the police." The shoe rested in the student's hand, raised slightly in front of us. We sat transfixed and in fear of her shoe—it had become a numinous presence from its former functional purpose. The student's imaginative recollection had transformed it before our eyes and ears. The dramatic unfolding in front of the room, wherein words and image congealed, left us all exhausted when she finished. Applause seemed grotesque. We all sat in silence for some minutes.

3. Poetics of Pity in Dante's Infernal Suicides

A third form of being present to violence is through one of the most violent poems in all of literature: Dante's *Inferno*, the first cantica of his *Commedia* written in the early part of the 14ᵗʰ century. I ask you to engage with me for just a few moments in concluding this essay, at the realm of the suicides, one face of those souls who did violence to themselves in life and now suffer its aftershocks for eternity— *animarum statem post mortem*—in the state of souls after death.

We pilgrimage as readers with Dante and his guide, the classical Latin poet, Virgil, into the 7ᵗʰ Circle, Second Ring, wherein suffer in strained desperation the violent against themselves. In their eternal condition, the souls of the suicides have been transformed into barren trees, which reflect poetically something of their deformed condition in life. The austerity of the terrain is stifling as the poet describes it for us: "no path had left its mark./No green leaves in that forest, only black;/no branches straight and smooth, but knotted, gnarled;/ no fruits were there, but briers bearing poison" *(Inferno* 13. 3-6). Perched on such barren branches are the mythical Harpies: "Their wings are wide, their necks and faces human;/their feet are taloned, their great bellies feathered;/they utter their laments on the strange trees" (13-15). Into such a landscape enter the living Dante and the shade of Virgil, slightly bewildered by the grotesque and austere landscape.

Disorientation, confusion and even paralysis consume the pilgrim; he hears the sound of cries but can see nothing. He ceases motion and in his posture becomes a suicidal tree, not unlike the woods surrounding him and his guide. The ecology of suicide is both disparate and desperate; nothing grows here, nothing flourishes. We should not miss the exhausted landscape and the violence that inhabits such a beleaguered region. Nor should we miss the confused state of such a disoriented soul who concluded that the only way to handle his irrefragable suffering was to self-murder. The confusion of Dante towards this landscape surfaces most clearly when he turns his attention to Virgil: "I think that he was thinking that I thought/so many voices moaned among those trunks/from people who had been concealed from us" *(Inferno* 13. 25-26).

What happens next displays a further insight into self-violence and its deeper psychological motives. Virgil encourages Dante to break from one of the nearby branches a small twig so that his own thoughts would be cut off. Dante obliges, but notice his exaggerated response to Virgil's words:

> Then I stretched out my hand a little way
> and from a great thornbush snapped off a branch,
> at which its trunk cried out: "Why do you tear me?"
> And then, when it had grown more dark with blood,
> it asked again: "Why do you break me off?
> Are you without all sentiment of pity?
> We once were men and now are arid stumps:
> Your hand might well have shown us greater mercy
> Had we been nothing more than souls of serpents." (31-39)

One hears in the lament of the soul the outlines of tragic irony. *Pity* and *mercy* are two words that seem strange issuing from the hissing branch of the violent against one's self, for in life they were incapable of showing themselves these same qualities of compassion. Notice too the confusion that is not just semantic disorientation as Dante does not really follow Virgil's directions to break off a twig; he breaks off a branch from a "great thornbush." His response is exaggerated, a hyperbole of the original directive. We must as readers wonder: would the response from the now-broken soul have been so pronounced if the break were more in keeping with a twig than a branch? Is this distorted relation between what one hears and what one does also a property of self-inflicted violence—an exaggerated response to what was smaller in fact, but in the fiction of one's life grew to enormity well beyond its measured reality? Is violence the expression and confirmation of the absence of due measure?

We are not done yet: the metaphor Dante now deploys to gather the kind of speaking of the suicide is worth our pause.

> As from a sapling log that catches fire
> Along one of its ends, while at the other
> It drips and hisses with escaping vapor,
> So from that broken stump issued together
> Both words and blood; at which I let the branch
> Fall and stood like one who is afraid. (40-45)

In fear, one is paralyzed, unable to function with the reasoned response that fear dissolves. Virgil, and I won't quote him here, apologizes to the shade, confessing to him that he overstepped his own bounds as guide by directing Dante to snap the branch off the soul's tree. It is one of the only places within the 62 cantos in which Virgil guides Dante, where his guide makes a false step, and it occurs here, in the arena of violence. Violence has the capacity to disorient, exaggerate and shatter proportion and convention in its response. Recollect if you will my Cretin friend in the labyrinth of his own anger who turned on me earlier. What did his own violent design do to him for the rest of the day?

Dante's wounding the shade, in inferno for eternity for its own violence against himself, and Dante's own exaggerated response, followed by Virgil's apology for overstepping his own boundaries as guide, reveals in a small but potent vignette the disorientation of violence as well as its revelatory nature; in fact, its disorienting mythos is the condition for its revelatory claims as it spreads out to infect others near by. Violence is then a form of wounding and just this wounding is an opening, both a breaking out of and a breaking into. Violence may be understood as a restricting force, a way of dealing with difference, but in its distortion of torquing something out of its natural shape, it can open to the super mundane to expose the hissing blood and words of a soul suffering the consequences of its own desperate response to a life grown bewildered and incomprehensible. Only one solution is it capable of conjuring, so shrunken is its field of options.

Dante's controlled, formed and shaped poetic expression of violence, in addition, encourages and insists on being reflected through, wherein we as readers—who are addressed no less than 22 times explicitly and many more times implicitly in the 100 cantos—are asked to bring our own narratives to bear on this remarkable scene, and to meditate on the various ways we have and may continue to commit suicide on ourselves in this life. Dante's scene reveals that violence has its own epistemic thrust in the world, its own way of being present over against others—the otherness of ideas, religious beliefs, economic propensities, status, power, prestige, who counts and who is discounted. When something or someone is discounted, it tends to move off the shelf with a bit more speed than those who are not.

One last note: it seems to me that violence is in one of its uniforms a vain but not necessarily recognized attempt, to eliminate, damp down, even oppress, ambiguity, paradox, ambivalence, doubt, uncertainty, confusion, multiple possibilities. Yet the above scene with the shade of suicide opens many of these arenas up in the state of souls after death. Dante's genius here is to reveal in the animated afterlife the qualities that violence normally strives to suppress. His poem reveals the relentless mystery of violence, its many-faced nature, and the absolute necessity to continue to peer into its unfathomable depths to uncover an archetypal constant in the soul to strike out towards one's self and others in service of a deeper revelation.

For this essay I avoided filling it with citations from sources on violence in order to allow more space for my own thoughts and for the student's powerful narrative. However, the following works have proven very helpful in grasping the contours of such a powerful force in psyche and culture that violence continues to be.

Endnote

[1] "Violent Designs: Imagining Violence as Physical and Fictional." Mythology of Violence Conference. Directed by Dr. Lori Pye. Pacifica Graduate Institute. Sponsored by the Foundation for Mythological Studies, April 4-6, 2008.

Works Cited

Alighieri, Dante. *The Divine Comedy*. Trans. Allen Mandelbaum. New York: Knopf, 1984.

Bailie, Gil. *Violence Unveiled: Humanity at the Crossroads*. New York: Crossroad, 1997.

Bok, Sissela. *Mayhem: Violence as Public Entertainment*. Reading, Massachusetts: Addison-Wesley, 1998.

Campbell, Joseph. *The Flight of the Wild Gander: Explorations in the Mythological Dimensions of Fairy Tales, Legends and Symbols*. Novato, California: New World Library, 2002. 27-42.

De Vries, Hent and Samuel Weber, EDS. *Violence, Identity, and Self-Determination.* Stanford: Stanford UP, 1997.

Diamond, Stephen A. *Anger, Madness, and the Daimonic: The Psychological Genesis of Violence, Evil and Creativity*. Albany: SUNY P, 1996.

Dostoevsky, Fyodor. *Crime and Punishment*. Trans. Jesse Coulson. Ed. George Gibian. New York: Norton, 1964. 1-466.

Ezekiel. Raphael S. *The Racist Mind: Portraits of American Neo-Nazis and*

Klansmen. New York: Penguin, 1995.

Favazza, Armando R. *Bodies Under Siege: Self-Mutilation in Culture and Psychiatry.* Baltimore: The Johns Hopkins UP, 1987.

Giegerich, Wolfgang. "Killings: Psychology's Platonism and the Missing Link to Reality." *Spring: A Journal of Archetype and Culture.* June, 1993, #54. Putnam, Connecticut. 5-18.

Gilligan, James. *Violence: Reflections on a National Epidemic.* New York: Vintage, 1996.

Girard, Rene. *Violence and the Sacred.* Trans. Patrick Gregory. Baltimore: Johns Hopkins UP, 1977.

Hamerton-Kelly, Robert G., ed. *Violent Origins: Ritual Killing and Cultural Formation.* Stanford: Stanford UP, 1987.

Jung, C.G. "Psychology and Literature." *The Spirit in Man, Art and Literature.* Vol. 15. *The Collected Works of C.G. Jung.* Trans. R.F.C. Hull. Bollingen Series. Princeton: Princeton UP, 1978. 84-105.

Kalsched, Donald. *The Inner World of Trauma: Archetypal Defenses of the Personal Spirit.* London: Routledge, 1996.

Maalouf, Amin. *In the Name of Identity: Violence and the Need to Belong.* New York: Penguin, 2000.

Mascia-Lees, Francis E. and Patricia Sharpe, eds. *Tattoo, Torture, Mutilation, and Adornment: The Denaturalization of the Body in Culture and Text.* Albany: SUNY P, 1992.

Mogensen, Greg. *God is a Trauma: Vicarious Religion and Soul-Making.* Dallas: Spring, 1989.

Nathanson, Donald L. *Shame and Pride: Affect, Sex, and the Birth of the Self.* New York: Norton, 1992.

Oliver, Mary. *New and Selected Poems.* Boston: Beacon, 1992.

Pinker, Steven. "Violence." *The Blank Slate: The Modern Denial of Human Nature.* New York: Penguin, 2002. 307-22.

Seltzer, Mark. *Serial Killers: Death and Life in America's Wound Culture.* New York: Routledge, 1998.

Strong, Marilee. *A Bright Red Scream: Self-Mutilation and the Language of Pain.* New York: Viking, 1998.

Travis, Carol. *Anger: The Misunderstood Emotion.* New York: Simon and Schuster, 1982.

Volf, Miroslav. *The End of Memory: Remembering Rightly in a Violent World.* Grand Rapids: William B. Eerdmans P., 2006.

Whitmer, Barbara. *The Violence Mythos.* Albany: SUNY P, 1997.

Whitmont, Edward C. *The Return of the Goddess.* New York: Crossroad,

1982.

Young, Dudley. *Origins of the Sacred: The Ecstasies of Love and War*. New York: Harper, 1992.

CHAPTER 6

BOXING PIETY'S SHADOW

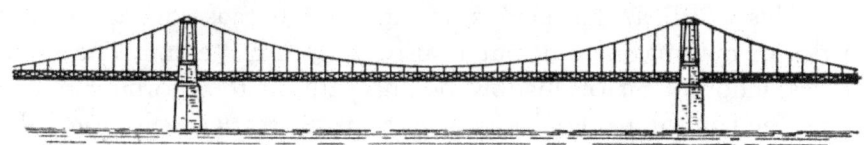

"Nicomedes, Bone-Gatherer"

Brazen towards discarded bones
you gave yourself to whips
lined with lead to beat the sacred
past your door into the
streets of Rome.

Bone-gatherer, picking the hard
shards of martyrs
placing them in a bag,
a marsupial pouch of sorts to create another
selfless self....

~Dennis Patrick Slattery, *Feathered Ladder* 107

Now that the elections of November are behind us, I believe a
moment of reflection is appropriate in order to consider one aspect

of the war between the United States and Iraq primarily, but reflection is certainly not limited to that incursion: the language of "axis of evil," the fundamentalist leanings of both sides of the agon, and the implicit and often explicit voice of piety claimed, uttered and appropriated by all factions involved, of which there are many. All of this turmoil and conflicting points of view, each claiming moral superiority, forces me to ask: What is the nature and presence, in various guises, of piety today? Even more to the point: in what disguises does the shadow of piety reveal itself in a communally psychological manner? What, in fact, does piety hide, camouflage, deflect, distort and indeed maim? The following pages reflect my attempt to muse on piety's subtle and clever disguises. Piety can launch a thousand ships as well as sink an entire nation's health and destiny.

This word *piety* has always unsettled me because of the cache it carries in my imagination, but I suspect I am not alone. The word invites action, a bit of shadow boxing early in the morning hours, under the light of a street lamp, always against a brick wall, where the shadow falls in ripples and refuses any chance of a knock down or knock out. Some bruising, though not life-threatening, is often the less harmful version of the consequences of both combatants' face-off.

Piety as a word often invites both skepticism and belief, gripping what one does not wish to relinquish and perhaps in other instances loosening the bonds of that same braided rope of convictions. Piety invites each of us to meditate on what we know and what we believe and to make some distinctions between the two realities that are often confused, at odds with one another, or in accord with one's basic tenets, or simply dismissed as irrelevant. When we learn in reading Virgil's classic epic, the *Aeneid* and find in those pages the epithet "pious Aeneas," are we startled, do we wince, or are we reminded of the power of this seldom used honorific?

Piety opens each of us up to the arena of basic moral and ethical ideas we gather about ourselves and our world. I wish therefore to begin with some thoughts about the nature of belief from a recent publication by the Spanish philosopher, Jose Ortega y Gasset: *What is Knowledge?* In one of the appendices, "Believing and Thinking," he includes a fine run at what beliefs are and how they differ from ideas. First Ortega establishes that the world and this "self" that a human being encounters appear to him or her under the guise of an interpretation, of "ideas" about the world and the self. This form of "idea," called by Ortega y Gasset "beliefs," are not in fact thoughts we neither have nor are they "occurrences" (178). Rather, these beliefs "form the container of our lives, and because of that, they do not exhibit the character of being particular contents *within* our lives. It is possible to say that they are not ideas we have, but rather, ideas we are" (178). Our beliefs place us in them, he goes on to reveal. So powerful is this insight that it has become a vernacular expression in Spanish: "estar in la creencia," to find oneself placed in a belief. A belief, then, "possesses us and gives us its support" (178). It is also a home, temporary or permanent, from which we peer out at the world and make sense of it through a specific place, the place in this case, of piety itself.

Ortega y Gasset's meditations on belief seem to me to offer a provocative compass bearing by which to explore the often craggy geography of piety. At least, such is my belief, which is a container for the ideas I want to pour into this essay vessel and stir a bit. It is another way or style of stewing over an idea. The proof may then pass the pudding and reside in where things are stewed up.

The word *piety* itself has a fascinating pedigree. It enters the English language in 1325 as *piete*: mercy, tenderness, pity and earlier as a surname *Piete*, according to my *Concise Dictionary of Etymology* (1195). Piety was borrowed from Old French *piete*, from archaic and colloquial Latin *pietatem* (nominative *pieta*, the source of Classical *pietas*) which suggested "dutiful conduct, kindness, pity, from the archaic and colloquial *pius*—source of *pias*, dutiful, kind (Pious) (567).

The Oxford English Dictionary records piety as "habitual reverence and obedience to the gods or God; devotion to religious duties and observances; godliness, devoutness. It further uncovers the word's meaning as "faithfulness to the duties naturally owed to parents, relatives; dutifulness, affectionate loyalty and respect" (2170). Thus reads a much abbreviated version of the word's ripening over time, catching as it travels through history certain nuances and shadings of both behavior and disposition.

What then, I ask, is the imagination of piety that surrounds me when I hear the word or say it? It carries, like all words, even parts of speech or even punctuation marks, a psychic energy for both the individual and the collective if they are properly attuned to its power.

I explore piety then, under the mantle of impiety's presence; perhaps such a cover will allow me, through resisting its charm, to see something of piety's innards, its shadowed sinewy self. Something sticky, unpleasant to the touch; perhaps piety has something up its sleeve I don't wish to touch, but I won't know that until I reach *out,* and then *in.*

Here is my stance: I need to allow piety's imagination to imagine me; then we'll see what's what. Maybe. I already feel dread returning, provoked by this "P" word. I sense its shadowy underbelly. No accident, therefore, that in volume 9,$_2$ of C.G. Jung's *Collected Works, Aion: Researches into the Phenomenology of the Self,* a discussion of shadow psychologically, follows immediately after his essay on Ego. Of course, to speak of piety from the angle or terrain or disposition of ego will yield only one face of piety. But if addressed from a more shadowed and moist alcove, I wonder if another facet of piety might surface and yield itself to a benevolent scrutiny? That is my hope. Where I stand within or beside a word has much to do with what it will yield. Is it possible, then, to deploy to the level of consciousness tenets of piety's shadow—historical, psychological, mythic, political, and theological?

Perhaps the appropriate question to pose at this juncture takes the following form: is piety an archetype? For Jung, archetypes are another way of speaking about mythological motifs, that is, typical modes or forms in which these collective phenomena are experienced ("The Fight with the Shadow" ¶447). Does it qualify? That is one possibility. Another: does piety fall under the shadow of an archetype? Or turn it a bit: can and do archetypes fall under the shadow of piety? If either is true, what then would they look like? Is piety one of the shards that lie quietly in the geographic plane and plan of history, of an historical consciousness, as well as in a collective unconscious, and so has been present with us from the beginning, as an impulse of the soul? Piety, understood as a psychic plant, an organic growth in the soul, then insists we consider what might unfurl from it, especially if watered by a certain set of beliefs, as well as by a particular relation of ego towards it. Is it even safe to have faith in piety? Can piety, in other words, be trusted? Is it, by contrast, its very seduction to be trusted that has made piety's shadow material so destructive on the global stage both yesterday and today?

I wonder then, if piety has a shadow cast by the shadow archetype? Is piety, in addition to all that has been said here, also a shady character—full of shadowy ridges, *cul de sacs* and surprises that might perturb with excess? You have noticed by now how shaky and uneven words can be in this pilgrimage towards and into piety. I wonder as well if the methods we use to research, our approaches to knowing, are not best listed among our own pieties? Our mythodologies may indeed be counted among our most treasured pieties. To think of this phenomenon politically, then ideologies are the worst form of piety, for they tend to leave no room for tolerating other forms of belief. Piety has the thorny power to foreclose on any beliefs or attitudes that are not, well, as pious as I want to insist on.

Jung delivered his chapter on the shadow to the Swiss Society for Practical Psychology in Zurich in 1928. There he wrote: "the shadow is a moral problem that challenges the whole ego-personality—no one can become conscious of the shadow without considerable moral effort" *(CW* 9,$_2$ ¶14). The shadow, he went on to claim, "is constituted by inferiorities. They have an emotional nature, a kind of autonomy and as such an obsessive or possessive quality" (¶15). So too with piety? Does it also cast a shadow, down through history, over millennia, across epochs, projecting its darker side that may become decree, mandate, cultural mythos, public policy, religious belief, and spiritual certitude, even a pesky and damaging ideology? History records examples of all of the above. Piety may harbor in its righteous robes a form of terror leveled at all who do not yield to a narrow set of standards as to its nature.

Piety may be envisioned, therefore, following Jung, not as something one is—pious—but rather a filter or colored glass by which one sees and perhaps shapes one's bundle of beliefs that comprise one's world view. As such, the light can refract a number of ways and some of those refractions can be destructive. In the reality of piety's shadow, it must be, as Jung observes of one's shadow material, fed daily to keep it going. Piety, as an unconscious force, deformed at times, gnarled at others, is the energy source, the turbine that keeps an individual, indeed an entire people, propelling forward. Piety therefore constitutes an essential block in the edifice of one's mythology, individual and collective. Later, in a radio broadcast through the BBC in November, 1946, and then in *Collected Works,* vol. 10, Jung reminded his audience of one simple rule to keep in mind:

"the psychopathology of the masses is rooted in the psychology of the individual" ("The Fight with the Shadow" ¶445).

In his thoughtful and insightful study of Christianity's heritage, the Benedictine monk, Bruno Barnhart, offers, to my mind, a superb historical summary of the Christian ethos in *Second Simplicity: The Inner Shape of Christianity*. In it he cites the theologian, Walter Brueggemann, who draws from successive stages of the Old Testament literature a scheme of three stages that aids Barnhart's own discussion of a critical shift from monotropic to a pluralistic Christianity. Monotropic Christianity is a form of belief which allows only one way of seeing in an authorized form (59). As a consequence, the natural richness and pluralism of Scripture is suppressed.

> Stage 1: The period of Torah, an original and authoritative unity. An unchallenged consensus based on divine Revelation.
>
> Stage 2: The time of Prophecy when this authoritative uniformity and general consensus is challenged by certain individuals, causing a break-up.
>
> Stage 3: Phase of Wisdom, the time of a new unity, but with a depth and breadth able to incorporate a wide diversity within itself.

At the source of this opening is a new experience of the presence of immanent and ubiquitous divine Wisdom, making all things one (59-60). We are, believes Barnhart, in the Second Stage today, the period of break up and break down, a clearing zone in time and space to allow room for something to grow up and out. In periods of breakdown, the shadow material of what has been working underground is invited, even coerced, to surface.

The following list of descriptions of piety's shadow may then highlight and even further this second phase; the consequences may open piety to a former nobility and even a wider acceptance. So to piety's underbelly, its shadowy profile:

- Piety may and has degenerated into a fundamentalist attitude, bereft of a symbolic order and absent depth.
- Piety transforms all forms of belief, thought and imaginings into replicas of itself. As such, its emphasis is on a blanket

veneer that destroys or ignores all differentiation, attention to and respect for, particularities.

- Piety degenerates into Pietism.
- Piety ripens, then rots into a belief in a single way of seeing, believing and being.
- Piety becomes fiercely judgmental, ferociously bent towards self-rightness and self-righteousness.
- Piety hides or blankets the shadow of a person or institution by canceling any form of serious self-reflection. One consequence of this movement is that the shadow of piety is exactly what the individual or the masses are seduced by.
- Piety checkmates self-critique in its single devotion to its own survival and growth.
- Piety forecloses on a diverse, multi-dimensional vision.
- Piety gains energy in a belief: there is only one way, mine/ours.
- Piety's power allows it to shape itself into its own divinity.
- Piety then breeds violence and force that drains all mythos from Logos—what remains is a dried husk of dogmatic assertions. In the same manner in which Jung asserts that "Peace is uncanny because it breeds war" ("The Fight with the Shadow" ¶456), so does the shadow of piety possess the same inclination to destructive disorder.
- Piety devolves into pomposity, a persistently pusillanimous pedagogy.
- Piety detaches itself, splinters off from a larger Logos and enthrones itself as divine arbitrator.
- Piety can create confusion between the finger—the instrument of pointing—and the moon—the object of its inclination.
- Piety abandons or abdicates the power of metaphor by literalizing belief.
- Piety eschews a sense of irony that protects and promotes a loose attitude of self towards one's self.
- Piety can become institutionalized in its manner of belief and so abandon its mythic and spiritual vitality.
- Piety decomposes into one source of truth as it adopts a form of existence *in vacuo*.
- Piety can transform mystery into dogma, wonder into

certitude and myth into calcified dogmatics.

- Piety can create further, or nurture, an attitude of dualism.
- Piety works diligently to protect exclusivity.
- Piety cancels verticality, depth and authentic reflection.
- Piety can widen, not diminish, the gap between nature and grace, God and the human person, divinity and secular heredities.
- Piety can rupture the energy flow between what is considered sacred and the human person.
- Piety can authorize a Jihadist sectarian destructiveness.
- Piety creates lacunae in consciousness.
- Piety's creation of its own energy field can pull all other forms of knowing into its stubborn and sustained orbit.
- Piety can establish with great subtlety our own frames of reference as **the** frame of reference.
- Piety has both the power and capacity to shape many forms of totalitarianism, however gnarled it might need.
- Piety has the capacity to transform all thought into feeling in a campaign towards mass conformity.

Piety, however, can and perhaps must, like a seed, descend, travel underground, there to decay and die. Then, once it dies to itself, it can bear fruit. Piety must go to ground. Then we will really have something. Exploring piety from this vantage point has earned the word in my lexicon a new level of respect. Devious means, deformity, decay, disintegration. Perhaps a form of the *via negativa* is also a fertile road into the image of piety and the fantasy that piety excites in us.

I keep close at hand James Hillman's powerful insight:

> Pathologizing is a way of mythologizing. Pathologizing takes one out of blind immediacy, distorting one's focus upon the natural and actual by forcing one to ask what is within it and behind it. (*Revisioning Psychology* 99)

Our way in is more poetic than political, more musing than mechanical, more circuitous than certain. Piety can handle it. The myth of piety's impulses, however, may suffer from such an irksome exposure. For my own work, piety is unboxed, more fully seen and more valuable because of this dubious debut, one which unsettles. That is my hope. What one fails to recognize in the force field of piety, as Jung observes about everything that is ejected or "disappears from one's psychological inventory is apt to turn up in the guise of a hostile neighbor who arouses your anger and makes you aggressive" (*CW* 10 ¶456). Rather than shadow boxing with piety, I would prefer to track its inward movement so that it reveals itself in a fuller splendor.

Endnote
[1] Paper presented at a Conference on Piety and the Enlightenment at the Dallas Institute of Humanities and Culture, Dallas, Texas, November 3-4, 2006.

Works Cited

Barnhart, Robert. *The Barnhart Concise Dictionary of Etymology.* New York: Harper Resource, 1995.

Barnhart, Bruno. *Second Simplicity: The Inner Shape of Christianity.* New York: Paulist P, 1999.

Boni, Allen *The Compact Edition of the Oxford English Dictionary*, Vol. 2. Oxford: Oxford UP, 1971.

Hillman, James. *Revisioning Psychology.* New York: HarperCollins, 1975.

Jung, C.G. "The Shadow." *Collected Works.* Vol. 9,₂. Princeton: Princeton UP, 1970. 8-10.

---. "The Fight With the Shadow." *Collected Works,* vol. 10. Princeton: Princeton UP, 1964. 218-226.

Ortega y Gasset, Jose. *What is Knowledge?* Trans. Jorge Garcia-Gomez. Albany: SUNY P, 2002.

Slattery, Dennis Patrick and Brian Landis. *Feathered Ladder: Selected Poems.* Iatook, Oklahoma: Fisher King Press, 2014.

CHAPTER 7

HESTIA: GODDESS OF THE HEART(H)

The stories we live and tell are ways of imagining our psychological and emotional lives, those pockets we inhabit daily. When we recognize and tell our stories we walk along a line that connects our narrative truth to our history and the figures in our story to myth. We also link in communion with the stories that listen to ours—others, stories we read and that reverberate with our own sonorous stories. A myth, as I understand it is an archetypal expression and enactment of a narrative, having its own logic, logos and plot.

But always we are guided by a pattern and a purpose, an image as well as an idea and an energy or power that holds the entire work together. James Hillman states this idea eloquently: "Inside our plans and projects lie motivations. Inside our ideas and methods of thinking are patterns that shape their logics. It is "as if" the laws of logic and language itself, submit to the rhetorics of imagination" (*Mythic Figures* 74). We may, then understand the figures of the gods and goddesses as emblems of strategies of thought and understanding as well as energy fields that reverberate value, meaning and significance. By means of them we perceive, assess, translate and interpret. Divinities aid us in forming our theories. Hillman amplifies: "these figures [are] forming influences giving a deeper archetypal validity and credence" (75) to our lives. One such figure that is the focus of this essay is Hestia.

She is, mythically, the daughter of Kronos and Rhea. In Barbara Kirksey's provocative and insightful essay on Hestia that informs my own thinking on this goddess, the author points out the paradox of Hestia; she is the oldest and youngest child of her parents in that "she was the first swallowed and the last to return from his stomach. Thus she is the first Olympian . . . but the most obscure" (*Facing the Gods* 103). Indeed, her history is enigmatic and often obscure. Connected to the figure of Kronos in this way, she is the figure of all time, of first and last, of beginning and ending. Moreover, she is of the earth; earth and time congeal in her. We need Hestia in time because she carries the seed of Kronos—of time itself—in our chronological life; she combines psychological life—the realm of myth—with chronological time—the realm of history and human temporality—and is thus the fullness of imagining that is mytho-historical as well as primally spatio-temporal.

My intention in this chapter, however, is to interrogate and imagine Hestia as a particular form of imaginal presence as well as an attitude, for divinities carry outlooks and styles of consciousness as much as they do any other qualities or characteristics, and with equal importance. I want to imagine Hestia, with the aid of Kirksey's essay, to feel what it is like to be in her presence and what she presents as a divinity of soul. I do not think any other god or goddesses takes us as close to heart and hearth-knowing as does Hestia. I also suggest that every god or goddess poses questions to us that take us, if we are willing to migrate out of our familiar terrain, into the center of our own personal myth.

The kind of focusing mentioned above is in fact perhaps the central attribute of Hestia: she is the goddess of concentration, of focusing, of paying close and sustained attention and of discerning and bequeathing value to this, not that, to what attracts, that feels significant and worth our attention. We need her desperately in an age of distraction, diversion and ADD-induced consciousness. To be attention deficit is to be without Hestia's power to focus long enough to deepen one's attention and understanding. ADD is then a form of orphaning our consciousness from the world soul. ADD is homelessness mythically; homelessness becomes more pronounced when we discover how Hestia is goddess of the home and the hearth fire that illuminates it.

Originally, as Kirksey informs us, Hestia was worshipped at the center of the city. The focus of the polis was the heart of the city, even the city's hearth as an analogue of the hearth of the individual home and the heart of the individual. This was true in the Greek world as well as in the Roman figure, Vesta, in their city. We might then ask: what is the nature of being at the center such that hearth-knowing becomes possible? We have historically very few images of Hestia; one of them that endures was as a "heap of live coals" (102). As the heart is the center of feeling in the human body, so is the hearth the center of focusing in the *oikos* (the household or home), as well as the polis. Indeed, home and city are connected intimately, if not with warmth, by the Hestian heat of the heart(h).

When I read of Hestia I begin to dream of the hearth: red-glowing warmth. In this attitude she is heart-feltness itself. In her presence one warms to one's subject matter, to situations, and to others with great care and concern. She is the energy that warms relationships, gives them heart. When we warm to another, either of long-standing or in new-found friendship, we have invited Hestia into the relationship, into the heart-shared between two persons. As one who warms hearts and hearths, Hestia congeals soul and place as well as gives one a local harbor and habitation. Further, her hearth presence restores warmth that has become absent in some cases; in doing so, she creates or refashions community, a sense of belonging, of being sheltered, and of membership in value. Her presence gathers random events into a common space and into a coherent story.

As the presence of co-herence she both invites and promotes wholeness. She is that invisible energy that helps to fashion an underlying form to a life and to narratives by allowing and persuading the various elements of a plot to gather in a poetic order. Without our narratives as rhetorical forms of mucilage to hold us together, we may wander homeless in the world, orphaned from the cohesive forms that keep us conscious of our identity as it evolves. In this way Hestia continues to bring us home and spares us from continually wandering.

Both in Greek and Roman myths Hestia's space is round, like the beautiful and elegant Vestal temple in the heart of Rome, a site my wife and I visited countless times when we lived there for two years. Its graceful roundness invited us to walk around to complete the circle. In the Vestal temple burns a light; legend has it that if the flame is ever allowed to extinguish, then Rome will fall. The flame at her Roman temple echoes the hearth fire of the home. It is where families and friends gather. At night, at a campsite, the central gathering place is the campfire; there all congregate, often sitting in a circle around the flame that allows all to see the familiar because the night envelope is held back. Kirksey writes that "the circularity of the hearth was the expression of sacred space" (105) and mirrors the shape of Gaia, earth herself. The circular hearth finds it companion in the contour of the planet; such is Hestia's wide-ranging embrace. To sit in the round, perhaps even to be well-rounded, is to enter Hestia's rich geometry, both personal and planetary.

Each morning when I rise early to read and write, after getting my cup of coffee, I enter my study, turn on one small light, then light a candle which is inevitably round. It is my homage each morning seven days a week to Hestia's possibilities that are invited into this quiet space by means of concentrating, meditating and focusing. When the light is not lit my thinking is off, I have difficulty concentrating, and my thoughts are less incisive, yes, less focused. Without Hestia's guidance I often waste my time in these precious hours before daylight. On this very point, I believe Hestia is also complicit in the acts of reading and writing, which I understand as two powerful forms of meditation. When I read or write in the intense glow of Hestian candle light, I feel my presence and my purpose each morning originating in the heart, not just the head. When I sit at times to simply gaze at the candle, ideas, images, insights inevitably visit me. Some are discarded while others become the rich prompt into a series of thoughts that lead me somewhere new. So Hestia may in fact be one of those gracious divinities of learning itself.

A virginal quality seems to be present early in the morning, unpolluted by the cares and responsibilities of the day. As a synthesizer, Hestia's flame illuminates virginal ideas; a purity of presence attends original thinking. She brings the virginal into secular space; the virginal in this sense is sacred, unpolluted, pure, unadulterated, clean in the sense of unfettered and undirty. Not that thinking, imagining cannot be messy, but that is not the same as polluted. Hestia may be the human impulse to stave off what is unclean from the unpolluted.

Something of this same magic happens when students in a class are willing to sit, not in rows with their vertical ambience, but in the round. Then we contain something and Hestia feels welcome as we assume her shaping influence. Students see one another's faces, not the backs of one another heads. The communication deepens when one can see the faces of others and be seen in turn. There seems also less distraction, more ability to attend to the matter at hand. Might the human face also be Hestian territory, with the eyes that shine, the face that glows, the expressions that warm, the voice that expresses, along with the face, the interior hearth of the person? So much of our bodies' heat gathers and exits from the head. Are we perhaps heated by Hestia in this way, where concentration holds the rest of the body's energy in an intense focus? I believe this is how we might imagine the heat of our own energy when we warm to an idea, or a key insight catches fire in us that torches into a complex vision of understanding. As such, Hestia is a fundamental power in learning itself as an activity both divine and human.

In one class I teach that never has more than four students, we begin each session with a ritual of lighting a candle and inviting Hestia to help us focus. To do so ritualizes the neutral secular space of the classroom into a sacred dwelling—a habitation that is human, focused, playful and intense the way a hearth fire is first intense before it slumbers back into a red glow that heats without flaming the inhabitants. Psychic space finds a home through the ritual. Now that she has joined us, we find ourselves being illuminated by one another's work read to the group. Then the student's essay becomes the light by which all of us see more into the subject matter than we would have ever achieved alone. Kirksey is so insightful at this point: "Within her pristine position, Hestia is able to *guard images*.... Hestia illuminates. Her illuminating provides protection and fostering of the image" (107). Perhaps the early Greeks felt there was some sacred, even divine quality, to the image so they assigned a goddess to hold it. In an imaginal way, Hestia amplifies the image, seeing by means of her illuminating prowess into the image's possibilities. Learning takes place precisely in this instant of amplification as well as protection.

On this note, perhaps we can venture that Hestia is very close and instrumental to the origin of myth, if you will entertain that myth is akin to a *via,* an avenue or corridor that promotes focusing. A myth can also include a particular style of understanding, of assessing value to something to make it more vibrantly present. What allows me to focus on anything is the myth I am in and perceiving by. My personal myth is like my home; from it I look out through very unique windows and doors onto the world. It is the home base of my illuminations, where I am lit up by an idea, like the light bulb over the cartoon character's head. That light bulb carries the wattage of Hestian illumination. It carries the energy of the Eureka moment that is such a delight when it occurs because it transports us to another home base from which to understand something new.

Kirksey further illuminates the rich complexity of Hestia by relating an insight by the Roman poet, Ovid. "Ovid tells us that the word for hearth in Latin is *focus* and 'the hearth *(focus)* is so named from the flames, and because it fosters *(fovet)* all things'" (107-08). To continue the ideas of myth stated above, what allows me to focus on anything is the myth I am in and perceiving by. What I focus on is mythos. Myth may be understood as a focal plane and a focal point. It is where energy gathers to make something meaningfully and often originally present. Hestia is a goddess of presencing, of bringing into view, of crossing and pausing in my field of vision. Any of us can experience moments in our lives where our trajectory, purpose and pursuits are all out of focus. Art, poetry, therapy, writing, painting, conversation are opportunities for regaining our focus, which is to say, our purpose. Absent any tincture of Hestia, a life can become out of control, unfocused, without direction and empty. We are not home *any place* under *any circumstances.*

Self-image may at times appear and feel distorted, indistinct or simply in opposition to our earlier image of ourselves. Sharpening our focus is a form of remythologizing our lives, infusing it with a clear purpose and vision. Kirksey believes that "returning to an image again and again from various directions is an attempt to focus—an attempt to find the fire of the image. This is imagining in a Hestian mode" (109). When we repeat a thought, an action, an attitude, it has a chance to grab hold, to inform us with ongoing energy. Hestia then is part of repetition, of pattern-constructing and maintaining. Writing, rewriting and revising are Hestian behaviors for in the re-writing one's focus sharpens; fire, light, illumination clarify, show boundaries and borders, make a crisp image rich and subtle; a certain clarity promotes nuanced and subtle seeing. Hestia helps us nuance the things of the world we focus on and find important, even indispensable. I would add that like writing and rewriting, reading and rereading are also Hestian; repetition to sharpen and deepen our understanding invites Hestia into such space. When we reread, for instance, we see details, connections, associations that the first reading skidded over and past. Rereading, I have found, is never just "re," a doing again; it is a movement into the unfamiliar because we are now familiar through the first reading of what is present; now we can focus on what was not there in that virginal reading.

Kirksey reveals at the end of her rich essay how Hestia joins two elements of human understanding back together that have suffered separation for millennia: imagination and perception. Together, they help to foster what she calls a central virtue of Hestia: "hospitality" (110). As the guest-host relationship is so central to the action of Homer's *Odyssey* as the wandering hero struggles to regain the hearth in his home with the assistance of his son and wife, Penelope, so does Hestia offer a rich and welcoming ground for ideas and images to be entertained. Being hospitable to ideas and opinions goes much further than being in opposition or at war with those that question or disagree with one's own. In making this connection with Homer's epic, I would venture that there may be present in the Hestian hearth presence the element of restraint, of pause, of holding back in order for what needs to present itself in its fullness to become apparent. It is a form of patience, of dwelling with rather than mastery over. Patience and restraint, of allowing time to host an idea, an image, another, seem to be Hestian attributes. The slow glow of the hearth fire is an apt metaphor for Hestian speed; it dwells rather than races, inhabits instead of darting here to there, and settles rather than scoots aimlessly.

Hosting ideas allows them the safe space to be voiced and heard; guesting ideas is the voice of the visitor, the newcomer, the one seeking to feel at home with his/her thoughts and opinions. Conversation, so absent in today's cultural sites, witnesses the presence of Hestian space and courtesy, a word whose etymology returns us to the heart. Courteous acts like listening and then speaking without attacking or colonizing the other's understanding evoke the presence of Hestia. In authentic conversation we adjust to the other's thought, insights, speech or writing; they in turn adjust to ours. Not agreement, but perhaps a certain consensus is the offspring of Hestian conversation. Hospitality is an opulent form of big-hearth-edness. It takes a large heart, or great-souledness, to listen with real attention to another without violating that space with one's overriding opinion or retort. Warming to the other's ideas is not synonymous with surrendering to them, or to pretend one agrees; rather, it is to allow the fire of their own perspective to infiltrate and perhaps modulate our own stance. Allowing such is a grandly hospitable endeavor that allows one to dwell with a contrary point of view in apposition, not opposition.

In his lead article, "On the Necessity of Abnormal Psychology: Ananke and Athene," James Hillman posits this bold and provocative insight: "What the Gods show in an imaginal realm of myth is reflected in our imagination as fantasy. Our fantasies reflect theirs, our behavior only mimetic to theirs" (3). Hestia, as an archetype of the imaginal realm, bestows on our own imagination a civility, a courtesy and a continuity because of her gifts of focusing, hospitality and hearthpitality. Without her, learning and human relationships would be flat, self-absorbed, static and in continual strife.

I think it is Hestia's dynamism, with her central image of the hearth fire that most animates my interest in her. She is less a goddess of acquiescence than she is of acceptance; less of yielding, more of a yearning; less hell-fire, more hearth-fire. When we notice that more of what surrounds us and dwells within us is placeless, homeless, orphaned—in thought, purpose, insight, voice—we may be drawn to light a candle to Hestia, to invite her in. She comes, I believe, by invitation only. When she shows up, be prepared to be a proper host so she can guest herself into our souls, there to kindle a fire that might have gone out without our even being aware of it. Her presence will spark gratitude in any who notice her.

Works Cited

Hillman, James. "On the Necessity of Abnormal Psychology: Ananke and Athene." In *Facing The Gods*. Dallas: Spring Publications, 1994. 1-38.

---. *Mythic Figures*. Introduction by Joanne H. Stroud. Vol. 6.1 of the

Uniform Edition of the Writings of James Hillman. Putnam, Connecticut: Spring Publications, 2007.

Kirksey, Barbara. "Hestia: A Background of Psychological Focusing." In *Facing The Gods.* Dallas: Spring Publications, 1994. 101-14.

CHAPTER 8

MYTH, METHOD AND MYTHOPOIESIS: JAMES HILLMAN'S ARCHETYPAL PSYCHOLOGY AS POETIC ARCHEOLOGY

Poetry is one of the destinies of speech.
~Gaston Bachelard, *The Poetics of Reverie* 5

In those limited occasions when I had the pleasure of speaking to James Hillman one-on-one, I would try to move the conversation along the lines of depth and archetypal psychology and poetry. I remember vividly when he arrived at the University of Dallas with Patricia Berry in the mid-70s, he quite explicitly showed great affection for the poets, poetry and literary classics. His co-edited volume with Robert Bly and Michael Meade, *The Rag and Bone Shop of the Heart*, offers further testimony to James' love of poiesis, in which the soul makes what it takes in into a form both coherent and creative as well as rich in its creatureliness.

He writes early in *Archetypal Psychology* (*AP*) in lauding the insights of one of his favorite poets, Wallace Stevens, that "there is always a poem at the heart of things" (34). In fact, he further proclaims that some of the most recent "explorations of archetypal psychology . . . have been in the direction of poetics, aesthetics, and literary criticism" (*AP* 35).

A full length study is needed to bring to substantial fruition the intimate connection between poetics and archetypal psychology, with the musing mucilage between them being myth; myth, to my mind is the nexus where the poetic and archetypal imaginations mingle with the metaphors between the two disciplinary realms—what might be called a psycho-poetics or mytho-poetics. Mythical figures then assume what might be called "as-if" presences, shapes that the psyche assumes as well as creates, to contribute poetic form to our psychological, embodied and emotional lives.

What James will deepen and extend from the insights of Jung on the nature of image, to which he alludes, is the nature of a "*fantasy-image,*" which Jung reminds us, "is related only indirectly to the perception of an external object" (*Collected Works* 6 ¶743). He refers to it, rather as an "inner image." Both writers implicitly and explicitly affirm that fantasy is an archetypal activity of the soul. Poetry, it seems to me, may be understood as an aesthetically crafted form of imaginal fantasy; its images open the soul to fantasizing, which is a form of interpretation. Hermeneutics is in part a creative process of fantasy creation; it resides in the space of analogy, metaphor, correspondence and accord. Both poetic as well as fantasy images are comprised in part of psychic energy, which in its activation give rise to patterns of awareness. Myth is what holds the patterns, endowing them with stability, durability and coherence. We make meaning in the act of reading, for example in our enjoyment of a classic of literature, a poem by Wallace Stevens or Jane Hirshfield, or an epic by Homer by entering the poetic images as they construct inner images in our own imagination. Some deep analogies are activated in our own dramatic unconscious that correspond to those aesthetically present in the work. Poetry is the formation, or in the thought of Gaston Bachelard's, *deformations* of imaginal realities (*Reverie* 81). Our own insights into the drama of our personal and collective mythology is given voice and coherence in such a process. These insights may comprise the third thing that Jung addresses as one contemplates images—poetic, fantasy, dream or reverie.

We might understand by this way of imagining literary figures in motion and laden with emotion, as forms of consciousness poetically rendered; they are mythopoetic in part because they have the imaginal muscle to infiltrate, incubate and initiate new ways of being conscious, in part by roiling to life images slumbering in the unconscious. "Imagining," suggests James, "means releasing events from their literal understanding into a mythical appreciation. Soul-making, in this sense, is equated with de-literalizing" (*AP* 39). Soul-making is an act; soul is the imagination of motion, or the motion of imagination to make into a new form what has been rendered in a particular and often distorted shape and form that insists on being renewed. Mytho-poiesis is then a poetic practice of bringing together bits and pieces of disparate parts into a new ordering of being using a more authentic and deeply enriched authority or claim. Poiesis offers an "as-if" property and proposition to perspective—it is an alternate way of believing, as myths themselves are optional ways of trusting the presence of the unseen. Jung repeatedly reminds us that when the images emerge, our best form of relating to them is simply to pay attention, to concentrate on them, to listen to them and to note their shifting associations: "It is very important to fix this whole procedure in writing at the time of its occurrence, for you then have ocular evidence that will effectively counteract the ever-ready tendency to self-deception" (*Jung on Alchemy* 89). Both Jung and Hillman give special regard to the process of soul-making as much as to the content that it offers us.

Another dimension of mytho-poiesis and archetypal psychology's relatedness reveals itself in placing actions, events, figures so that where they belong "by means of likeness, the analogy of events with mythical configurations" is a first step to cultivating an "archetypal sensitivity that all things belong to myth" (*AP* 49). Something here resonates with the fundamental nature of narrative itself. If a story line, its plot, its mythos in Aristotle's sense that James cites in *Healing Fiction* (11), can be understood as home, as our own narrative identities offer us a domicile to spare us from migrating from orphanage to orphanage throughout our lives, then to discover the lineages of likenesses establishes a place from which to understand what the terms of our plot include, where the parade of images begin to cohere into a comprehensible story, one we can believe in and cultivate further. It is an important curative step towards a *Healing Fiction*.

Deformation and affliction are two additional conditions that inform both archetypal psychology and poetics. Each, as James insists, carries its own way of imagining (*AP* 50). In poetry as well, we are given to imagine just such a pathological awareness through the properties of the plot that guarantee conflict, antagonisms, agons and agonies. Such a necessary recipe for having a story at all finds respite here and reveals pathos in prose; or poetic utterance offers the reader an instance of soul-making, not just in the act of being read or observed, but in the inner affliction of the audience members. Poetry deforms through an aesthetic form, some element or attitude the soul yearns for but may deny or deflect in the service of homeland security. The infirm are halted at the gates; the price tag is that the individual is left safe but uninformed. Infirmity contorts, twists, suffers, strains, bends human life into an exaggeration or into an exceptional expression. Poetry's pathos perpetuates a perspective of suffering that nurtures. We would seem to need and require poetry to help us engage our own individual patho-poetics.

Perhaps most intimate in the assemblage between archetypal psychology and poetry is where the literary theorist and critic Louise Cowan and James' work is most apparent and rich in their cross-fertilizations to create a new organic species of interpretive imagining. Those of us who have had the privilege of studying with either or both Louise and James, know that for Louise the genre wheel, consisting of the four "kinds" of poetry—Lyric, Tragedy, Comedy and Epic—are metaphors for the essential landscapes of the soul's motion. Now while James' categories differ in some ways from Louise's descriptions, they share a common denomination. James writes that "genres or categories of the literary imagination—epic, detective, comic, social realism, picaresque—become relevant for understanding the organization of narratives told in therapy" (*AP* 56). He then points us to Patricia Berry's keen insight: "the way we tell our story is the way we form our therapy" (qtd. in *AP* 56), which returns us to the beginning of this essay: "the entire procedure of therapeutic work must be reconceived in terms of the poetic basis of mind" so that we can "become conscious of the fictions in which the patient is cast and re-write or ghost-write, the story collaboratively by re-telling it in a more profound and authentic style" (*AP* 56). The soul's own unique style of expression is big enough a topic for a conference of its own.

By analogy, then, reading classic works of literature is an imaginal act of reclamation: we pay close attention to what draws us most poignantly to itself in figure, action or motive that bumps up against our own personal myth. We pay attention to the impulses to underline a passage, to write in the margin, to see what extension from the action we might take it to give a fuller meaning to our own fictional fixations and findings and then finessing our way towards a fuller notion of what characters we are as a blend of tendencies and fantasies. As readers, we spiral into and out of the interactive field of images in motion, acting out as well as being taken in. It is a double spiral—inward to the imaginal landscape of the poem, outward and then inward into our own narrative identity. Such a spiralic movement suggests the act of reading is like a drill bit; it bores down, grips on, holds fast, then backs out in a counterclockwise motion. Perhaps a ritual or rite of passages is appropriate in which we unscrew ourselves from a poem after we have screwed ourselves in, screwed up an interpretation, or even felt screwed by the plot that does not satisfy or that we have failed to drill deeply enough into, perhaps hitting a knot in the pine of prose that snaps the bit and stops our descent. We repeat the drill in rereading and find ourselves just a bit deeper into the narrative's mythic mystery at the center.

To further his connection between archetypal psychology and poiesis, James returns to the fundamental image of personality and re-news it: "Rather, personality is imaginatively conceived as a living and peopled drama in which the subject 'I' takes part but is neither the sole author, nor director, nor always the main character" (*AP* 63). In fact, this figure is multiple, contradictory, paradoxical and multi-intentioned. When we read literary works, then, we take in all the characters, not just our favorite or a small number, for each has the capacity to mimetically link with us, as re-presentations of our own psychic imagery. James will later refer to "participatory awareness" as "the primary qualifier of consciousness" (*AP* 73), proposing, in my view, that we create a mimetic link or identity with the characters in a literary work as part of the tissue of our own consciousness. Reading in this attitude is a therapeutic act wherein we "instead of" ourselves into the fictional fabric of a story that appears both like and dissimilar from our own. Such is the potent gravity of mytho-poiesis to generate such a union composed of differences.

Poetry is foundational to the imaginal work of archetypal

psychology, as James reminds us often in his writings: "Poetry plays an unusually significant role in the background of archetypal psychology" (*AP* 77); part of that importance resides in the metaphorical and mythical dimensions of language to substantiate a world that touches deeply the fictional nature of our own narratives. Literary genre theory, shared by James and Louise, is imperative for two reasons: 1. Through reading poetry and developing a poetic basis of mind, one also, like the practitioner of archetypal psychology, associates "myths in life to the recognition of life as myth" (*AP* 80); 2. The study of both myth and poetry, or what I have been calling mytho-poiesis, has as its intention "the transformation of insight" (*AP* 80). Both of these intentions, it is important to note that, for James, are beyond the "literalism of the personal" (*AP* 80). Not all about me; rather, all about beyond me, but nevertheless by analogy implicating me imaginally through the metaphors that I am, espouse, esteem and imagine forward.

Finally, but perhaps initially, James ends *Archetypal Psychology* by noting that Gaston Bachelard's poetics is more foundational to the work of archetypal psychology than are theories of phenomenology or systems primarily because "There is an elemental reverie, a mythical imagining going on in the world's stuff much as the soul of the human is always dreaming its myth along" (82). Therapy includes poiesis as much as aesthesis—a making of the beautiful in its most potent and promising appearances. One of James' major contributions in this slim volume, but with its tendrils extending into many of his other works, is in bridging the fictions of a life with the richness of poetic logos, and to claim for the fullness of the person the impersonal presences that guide us in their invisible but deliciously potent, wisdom traditions.

Works Cited

Bachelard, Gaston. *The Poetics of Reverie: Childhood, Language, and the Cosmos.* Trans. Daniel Russell. Boston: Beacon P, 1969.

Hillman, James. *Archetypal Psychology.* Uniform Edition 1. Putnam, Connecticut: Spring Publications, 2004.

---. *Healing Fiction.* Barrytown, New York: Station Hill P, 1983.

Jung. C.G. *Psychological Types*. Rev. by R.F.C. Hull of the trans. of H.G. Baynes. *The Collected Works of C.G. Jung. Vol. 6*. Princeton: Princeton UP, 1990.

Salant, Nathan Schwartz (Editor). *Jung on Alchemy*. *Encountering Jung Series*. Princeton: Princeton UP, 1995.

CHAPTER 9

WHAT IS MYTH AND THE GOD-IMAGE?

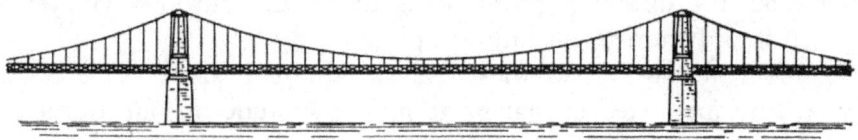

The ego participates in God's suffering. We have
become participants in the divine nature. We are the
vessel…of the Deity suffering in the
body of the "slave."
~C.G. Jung, *Nietzsche's Zarathustra*, qtd. in
The New God Image 75

My hope is that this talk[1] will serve a dual purpose: to describe some characteristics or attributes of what I call our personal myth, and to offer some remarks on the God-image, not God. I am not certain that God can be known; but God images are accessible to us. The image of God we carry within and are guided by is an intimate aspect of our personal myth, so the two topics are indeed related. First, let me tell you a story that will illustrate the voice of my own personal myth.

My wife and I had decided to walk part of the Camino de Santiago in Spain in September 2012. We prepared for a year, taking long walks around our neighborhood and, for a short time, carrying our backpacks filled with bags of flour to strengthen our bodies for the pilgrimage. We had decided to walk the 200 miles from Leon, Spain to the town of Santiago de Compostela. We allotted one month for this trek and planned to stay in hostels along this ancient of paths, used for centuries by the Romans and other people across Europe. Today it is one of the most popular pilgrimage routes on the planet.

We arrived in Madrid and spent two days there adjusting to the area and recovering from jetlag. One morning we then trained to Leon, about three hours from Madrid. There we rented a room in a convent for the night; next morning at 4 a.m. we, along with scores of other pilgrims from around the world, began our walk through the street-lamp lit town. All of us seemed to have agreed to walk in silence; most all of them set a pace that was far more brisk than our own. We reached the edge of town at dawn and left the streets and sidewalks for dirt and gravel roads that sliced through vineyards, orchards and enormous sunflower plots.

My wife Sandy had walked ahead about a quarter mile as we were both interested in making room for solitude on our journey. I shuffled along behind her trying to adjust to a backpack that, I knew already was far too overloaded. As I walked, however, a voice came to me with such assertion that even now I can still feel its presence: it came from behind me on my right side. The voice had only three words for me, but they carried such a shocking insight that they set the tone and the trajectory of the pilgrimage from that moment on. The words were: "Let Life Happen." And then the connection went silent. I was a bit stunned and yet strangely satisfied with the truth claim of this pronouncement.

A bit bewildered at first, I began, slowly, to examine all the ways in which I tried to control life, to make it fit into my narrow corridor of understanding how the world should work by following what I laid out as essential and desirable. I knew the voice had hit home with those three zingers that occupied me each day of the trip. Now, the source of the voice is open for discussion. I like to think it was the voice of St. James, or Sant-Iago himself, and he had tapped very quickly into a seminal staple of my personal myth. Part of my myth's manifesto had to do with control. The three words were the presence of liberation, antibodies of sorts, to counter the powerful poison that control insinuates into us. To "Let Life Happen" was to yield control to Life itself in all its mysterious unpredictability. I have, I believe, made some progress along that gravel road in my life. At the time of the voice's intrusion into my life walk I was approaching 68 years of age.

The Swiss psychiatrist C.G. Jung believed that the first half of life emphasizes our engagement with the outer world, with creating a life, cultivating a career, perhaps beginning a family; the second half of life, however, was a time of inward-turning where matters of the spirit become more pronounced and begin to gain ascendency over the concerns of life's first half. I believe the voice of insight I experienced was also directing me towards a deeper engagement with what I had been negotiating daily, but now on a deeper level of awareness. For many of us, our spiritual life is a central piece of our overall mythic complexion.

When we look closely at 12 Step Recovering Programs to counter many forms of addiction, we see that they are largely in service of developing a spiritual sense of self, what I call a unique spiritual identity. That movement is a painful one for many because it means giving up our habitual self-absorption and giving over our will to a Higher Power. Whatever God image is birthed here is the one that is supposed to help, not hinder, one's path to a greater spiritual awakening.

It is evident to me that our spiritual life is part of a larger mythic structure that is at once both personal and collective. Let us then look at some of the qualities and characteristics that comprise a personal myth. It contains:

- Patterns of awareness
- What I believe about myself and the world, which will influence what I believe to be true
- Prejudices that shape or torque the world into agreeable patterns
- The stories we tell that define us most emphatically
- Shadow material we might rather not face
- The entire mountain range of our emotional life
- What we enjoy doing and what we enjoy retreating from doing
- What comprises our "as-if" sense of ourselves and others
- Images we carry of ourselves and the world
- What we choose to remember

- What we choose to forget
- Energy fields of consciousness that shift, intensify, diminish to allow for certain elements to enter, others to be denied ingress (*Riting Myth* 19).

Now to ground all of the above, let's go to one myth we carry: our God-image within that guides our thoughts, behavior, needs and desires. I use the word "image" here so as to differentiate speaking or attempting to define what cannot be known from the image or images that can be discerned. The way we form our God-image is directly related to our personal myth. The cultural psychologist, Thomas Moore, cites in his recent book, *A Religion of One's Own* the medieval theologian Meister Eckhart, who wrote: "I pray to God to get rid of God" (*Religion* 15). Moore goes on to write shortly thereafter: "I'd rather live with glimpses of God than sightings" (16). I think that the word "God" takes us to religion, but "God-image" steers us toward psychology and mythology.

In his controversial and very exciting study, *After God*, theologian Mark C. Taylor advances in his Introduction another approach that may make sense to many of us: "In a world where to be is to be connected, absolutism must give way to relationalism, in which everything is codependent and coevolves. After God, the divine is not elsewhere but is the emergent creativity that figures, disfigures and refigures the infinite fabric of life" (xvii-xviii). Such a vision of faith and belief takes us out of an earlier notion that God is somewhere "out there" controlling, reinforcing and judging each of us. Today a more humanistic theology seems to be gaining ascendency to bring God closer to home. There is nothing simple about one's faith and in what form of God-image that faith worships and depends on. We do know that given the current strife in many parts of the world over various interpretations of God, faith and belief, we can assume that the topic is powerful enough to provoke myriad forms of violence, all in the name of a God-image.

So we ask at this juncture a series of questions that you may find useful in exploring your own myth's God-image:

- What form does your God-image assume in your life?
- Is it approximately the same image you carried when you were 11? 15? 35?

- If this image has changed over time, can you describe how it has morphed and what forces persuaded this change?
- Are there ways in which you acknowledge and even converse with your God-image?
- Does this image assume importance in your life because you feel a consistent desire to "be" within a spiritual life?
- Does your God-image grow in part from a feeling that physical nourishment, possessions and a comfortable life are no longer sufficient to sustain you at this moment in your life?

The mythologist Joseph Campbell claims in one of his books that the fundamental purpose of a myth is to serve as a transport vehicle by which we are moved to a place in our lives where "we become transparent to transcendence" (*Thou Art That* 18). Illness can transport us to this place; a divorce can bring us to this place; the loss of a loved one can drive us to this place; loss of connection with others can bring us to this place; a shift on our life-outlook can as well. Many others you could name. He went on to offer us a three-part journey that he assembled from his years of studying literature and world mythologies, one that is personal, psychological and spiritual:

1. The literal
2. The mythical
3. The mystical

Each of these realities builds on the one before. He remarked as well of the possibilities in being called to the world and at the same time into one's own interior cosmos:

- The call to the sacred is a frequent call
- Some do not hear it, by choice or by distraction
- Some hear it but choose not to heed it
- Some hear it, heed it and submit to it
- Heeding it, one chooses to give oneself over to something bigger than oneself

We might therefore ask of the religion we practice, presumably in the service of one's God-image:

- Does it help me further liberate myself from self-absorption and self-molesting?
- Does it help me to serve others and the world in a more generous capacity?
- Does it keep me chained to guilt, resentment, narrow prejudiced thought, fear-based feelings and behavior that embodies them?
- Does it serve as a buffer so I no longer even have to think about it?

These are all as much mythological questions as they are psychological in inflection.

In addition, both personal myth and our God-image or images are enacted in the world through rituals. The word needs a bit of description:

- Rituals are incarnated ways, both formal and informal, by which we remember what is important to us as well as a way to acknowledge those vital elements' integrity in our lives
- Rituals are forms of investing in the present/future by recognizing and enacting aspects of our present/past
- Rituals are both personal and collective. For instance, our birthday is personal, but Memorial Day and Labor Day are collective
- Rituals are religious responses to mysterious acts that we cannot fathom rationally
- Rituals are human impulses to keep soul present in parts of our past
- Rituals are ways of sacralizing history right now, on this date and time each year so that the event shaped into ritual becomes bigger than itself, even immortal, joining the pantheon of the gods or goddesses in our lives
- Rituals acknowledge and witness our religious and spiritual lives

Allow me to be concrete through an illustration in which a ritual enacts a particular attitude and a disposition towards a work. Each morning I enter my study at 4 a.m. seven days a week. I have enacted this ritual for 23 years. In my study rest quietly on the shelves hundreds of books that I will consult, but more importantly, I want to be surrounded by when I read.

I bring with me my morning coffee into the dark space illuminated by only a small desk lamp by my lounge chair. After turning on the light, I light a candle and on some mornings, a stick of incense. I love the aroma as it softly fills the room. The candle is to invite in and honor the goddess Hestia, who, among her other powerful attributes, is the goddess of focusing. As goddess of the hearth, she brings with her a sense of centering as well, as the hearth was often the center of the household before it was replaced by the white light of the television screen.

I then pull up from the floor next to my chair my journal, which I use to remember the day before; I wait quietly, not forcing any memories from yesterday but allowing them to emerge in whatever order they choose. What appears I write down without censoring any of it. I add my thoughts that wish to be associated with it, as well as feelings that attend the recollection. Writing these thoughts and remembrances takes no more than 20 minutes.

I then pull from the floor a three ring notebook which contains some 86 handwritten pages on Buddhist thought and meditation. It also contains dozens of handwritten notes from the pages of a book on adult children of alcoholics. I know that my ritual of life includes coming to a deeper understanding of the world I grew up in. I find this study reassuring. If, in the process of reading over a few pages of the notes, a line from a poem comes to me, I write it down and move on. Similarly, if a dream from last night or the night before arrives in this early morning hour, I write down what appears, if only in fragments. Recollection is the central theme in this first hour of being awake; never has material not arrived in the almost two dozen years of this meditative practice.

I often then pick up a book on spirituality or psychology for further meditation and take down ideas in note form. A few recent titles include Mark Taylor's *After God,* Thomas Moore's *A Religion of One's Own, Thomas Merton on Contemplative Prayer,* and Evelyn Underhill's *Practical Mysticism.* Entering one or another of their worlds places me in a certain disposition for the day. When this ritual is interrupted, something incomplete enters the day and rides through it until sunset.

I find that writing in longhand slows down the momentum of the day and places me more squarely and deeply in whatever subject matter engages me. There is in the spiralic geometry of cursive writing, which I have learned recently is being dismissed from public school curricula nationally, a power and sensibility that typing detracts from. Such has been my experience. When I read not long ago of C.G. Jung's observation that "all psychological development is spiralic" (*Dream Analysis* 100), it confirmed for me the importance of sensing and enjoying the slow drag of the pen across paper as a journey having its own beauty, force and resistance.

I end this portion of my day with a question that may be spiritual, psychological and mythical at once: "What is it that makes me wonder?" I ask this each day and am often astonished at the responses that emerge rather quickly. A few prompts also seem to aid the process of deepening, which is where wonder takes me.

- When have I had a glimpse of something else? Of knowing something in an intuitive or instructive way?
- When have I experienced a breakthrough or a breaking through to another level of awareness, understanding or insight?
- Who or what is it that I feel a deep sense of gratitude for?

These questions can lead to authentic moments of spiritual liberation; without them life may feel less full or rich, less of a fascinating pilgrimage.

I leave you with a challenge: try journal writing in longhand for one month, at least 5 days per week. Limit yourself to 20 minutes per day, at a time when you feel most relaxed, attuned and porous to outside and inside presences. See what, if any, benefits derive from doing it. If none, then let it go; if some, then try it for a second month. For many of you I believe it will transform into a regular part of your life and allow you to leave a record as a legacy of what you deemed important both mythically and in relation to your evolving God-image.

Endnote

[1] This essay was presented to the San Antonio Unitarian Universalist Church on July 20, 2014.

Works Cited

Campbell, Joseph. *Thou Art That: Transforming Religious Metaphor.* Ed. Eugene Kennedy. Novato, California: New World Library, 2001.

Edinger, Edward F. *The New God-Image: A Study of Jung's Key Letters Concerning the Evolution of the Western God-Image.* Ed. Dianne D. Cordic and Charles Yates. Wilmette, Illinois: Chiron P, 1996.

Jung, C.G. *Psychology and Religion: East and West. The Collected Works of C.G. Jung.* Vol. 11. Trans. R.F.C. Hull. Princeton: Princeton UP, 1977.

---. *Dream Analysis: Notes of the Seminar Given in 1928-1930.* Ed. William McGuire. Bollingen Series XCIX. Princeton: Princeton UP, 1984.

Moore, Thomas. *A Religion of One's Own: A Guide for Creating a Personal Spirituality in a Secular World.* New York: Gotham Books, 2014.

Slattery, Dennis Patrick. *Riting Myth, Mythic Writing: Plotting Your Personal Story.* Skiatook, Oklahoma: Fisher King P, 2012.

Taylor, Mark C. *After God.* Chicago: U Chicago P, 2007.

CHAPTER 10

AESTHETICS, POLITICS, ETHICS: AN EMERGING TRINITY OF IMAGINATION IN JAMES HILLMAN'S *CITY AND SOUL*

Books often surprise us by the way they find a way into our literary and personal lives. One such title that I cannot even recall how or when it was brought into my view, is by Henry A. Giroux, currently holder of the McMaster Chair for Scholarship in the Public Interest at McMaster University. The title is provocative and disturbing: *The Violence of Organized Forgetting: Thinking Beyond America's Disimagination Machine.* At this writing I am still reading it, but I have been thinking of some of his insights in relation to James Hillman's perspectives on politics and aesthetics. Here is a sampling of Giroux's thought early on. He has just been reviewing and lamenting the dissolution of democracy as an ideal in American life since the 1970s; he offers this conclusion:

Schools, libraries, the airwaves, public parks and plazas, and other manifestations of the public sphere have been under siege, viewed as disadvantageous to a market-driven society that considers noncommercial imagination, critical thought, dialogue, and civic engagement a threat to its hierarchy of authoritarian operating systems, ideologies and structures of power, domination and control. (32)

Beside Giroux's commentary on a number of places that imagination lives, such as education, art and liberal learning, is James Hillman's belief that aesthetics is necessary for a culture to flourish:

The word for perception or sensation in Greek was *aesthesis,* which means at root a breathing in or taking in of the world, the gasp, "aha," the "uh" of the breath in wonder, shock, amazement, an aesthetic response to the image (*eidolon*) presented. In ancient Greek physiology and in biblical psychology the heart was the organ of sensation: it was also the place of imagination. (36)

Some of his most insightful writings on aesthetics and its necessity for the health of culture are contained in *City and Soul.*
In 2009, in 14 provocative and often witty conversations with Sonu Shamdasani in *The Lament of the Dead: Psychology after Jung's Red Book,* he returns to this major staple of his thought and its close relation to poiesis, to the poetics of soul, to the making or shaping of a life mythically inflected and imaginatively slanted. In a current cultural paralysis that speaks only of one's economic state of being, Hillman insists that we must have the courage to stand up for our "aesthetic sense" as an antibody to the "pall of numbing conformity [which] deadens our language, our food, our work-places and city streets" (145). When an individual or an entire population suppresses the aesthetic response, "we leave the world to itself and isolate ourselves from its plight" (149). World rebuilding cannot occur without a major virtue that aesthetics promotes and undergirds: Trust. To lose trust is to deny or reject the aesthetic response; further, we lose trust in the animal sense of things, the way and intensity of things, people, objects in the world attract or repel us. Blunting such a crucial faculty of culture seems a major intention of the engineering, intense and relentless, taking place today to fashion a new myth, one which denies critical and aesthetic responses, the

ability to discern and the exercise of taste. Hillman saw this coming well before many of us even noticed it as a green blip on the screen; he wrote his way towards heading it off before the debacle of disposability that laces today's consumer culture dug into the soul's soil. Noticing, seeing clearly, paying attention to the details and particularities of things, objects, ideas, images italicize an aesthetic presence as well as stimulate a form of awareness that weds once more ethics to aesthetics. Separated, as they are today, both fall into oblivion or are maimed into disuse. United they command; divorced they cripple:

> I'm suggesting that all our ethical concerns for justice and fairness, for decency, require as well an aesthetic vision, such as images of the biblical and classical ideals of Jerusalem, the city on the hill, Zion, the restoration of the Temple, the image of Athens and its Acropolis, the cities of the Renaissance like Florence and Venice, images of Paradise, of Eden. (152)

Moreover, and coupled with aesthetics and ethics is language itself in both its eloquent and infirm conditions. Words themselves carry soul; it is part of Hillman's frequent mantra: to develop a poetic basis of mind, which is to speak such a poiesis in a language that enjoys and employs health, stamina and freshets of phrase. One might look then to the health of language in its freedom from clichéd expressions, worn out locutions, conventional knee-jerk sentences, sound-bites, and unconscious use of anemic metaphors to glean the soul illness of a people, a city and a civilization. It is one measure to learn to observe; it is quite another to find renewed language, free from group-speak, up-talk, up-chuck and the dead mutton of exhausted words that comprise another form of the malady of "psychic numbing," a term Hillman borrows from the cultural historian Robert J. Lifton.

In the chapter, "Natural Beauty Without Nature" in *City and Soul,* he argues against separating beauty from the quotidian order of things: buildings, fence posts, drinking fountains, fish aquariums, graffiti and pop music. Placing beauty in nature or in a painting misses the point of aesthetics that underlies beauty. He therefore unfurls a series of proposals to help with "disentangling the need for beauty from the need for nature" . . . so to cease splitting "the natural from the urban" (166). We sense Hillman's deliteralizing impulse here as his imagination deconstructs what we have accepted as formal properties of places like "nature" and "wilderness." By contrast, he envisions beauty occupying an ideal wilderness, as one example among many; this way of imagining "can be fostered by the attitude of walking the world without injury to it, leaving no trace, no leftover actions to be dealt with by others, giving priority to the physical thing over the subjective will" (170). We sense here an enactment of beauty, a nascent sense of ethics and political action as ecological awareness all at once. Also, and not least present, is an attitude of humility, of humus, of humane treatment of the particulars to allow them the dignity to flourish. I find most fascinating here and elsewhere his process of seeing down, into and through as reclamation of not just an earlier economy but an earlier mythic sensibility toward all things. Ecology then assumes the garment of psychological aesthetics.

He soon opens to lamenting the absence of beauty's discussion in therapy: "and the aesthetic plays no role whatsoever in therapeutic practice, in developmental theory, in transference" (174), nor in successful or failed therapy or when it terminates. Moving to a wider lens, Hillman's lament drills further to embrace the world's condition as it is as well as the chronic lapse in remembering that beauty attends it in many ways no longer noticed, witnessed or cultivated. Beauty, as we continue into his forest of examples and illustrations, is a mucilage of the soul that holds the world together in a particularly organized way. Ignoring or debasing such a quality or attitude under the mistaken idea that it really does not matter, affects the very way we see matter and make certain elements in our personal lives matter, what he will soon call the world's "inherent radiance," which "lights up more translucently, more intensively within certain events" (178).

His claims grow bolder in the section where he thinks mythologically by honing in on Aphrodite's presence in the world; actually she is more "a sense of the world" as a form of divine enhancement (179). She brings the world into a kosmos, which Hillman translates as "fitting order, appropriate, right arrangement, so that attention to particulars takes precedence over universals" (180). It also includes, as he continues, "the appearance of fittingness of each thing as and where it is, how well, how decorously, how appropriately it displays" (181). Such an ordering principle, the impulse to display in arrangement and coherence, is as I understand it the heartbeat of what myth itself leads us to meditate on.

Chapter 18, "The Cost of the Ugly," goes to the other side of beauty's existence as well as its absence. It carries its own high price tag not just for beauty, but for ethics and the interior ceilings of one's psychic life: "If the first cost of ugliness is depression, the second cost may be the degradation and violence of youth owing to anesthetized school budgets, budgets that cut back or cut out the arts" (197). Now here is the Hillman that I love, at work in making analogies where many of the rest of us—read "me"—would not see the psychological linkage. If school architecture inserts function over aesthetics, then one should not be surprised if such an environment where students spend their most productive hours creates dysfunctional children (198). So where is the hunger for aesthetics fed and, more, where does aesthetics connect to ethics?

Hillman's brilliance is to see the benefits in one of the most marginal forms of fear in our society, street gangs, resuscitating not just beauty but its relation to an ethic, a code, a form of behaving that while not accepted by a larger public, works very effectively within the backdrop of gang membership and the streets. "Appreciate the display: the hairstyles, tattoos and piercings, the attention to dress, the value of shoes, of jackets, the rapid transit of fashions. Listen to the beat in the language, watch the dance in the walk, the formalities of greetings, the words that indicate an eye for style, elegance, display. Show for its own sake. Aesthetics" (198). Notice here Hillman's own *aesthesis*: Aphrodite in the specific details, a scent of Helen's beauty in the particularities, the poetics of the rhythm of his language. The end-stopped fragment—show for its own sake. The last word, standing defiant by itself: "aesthetics" (198). His poetic genius, his mytho-poetic couplings, links the mythology of gangs to their revisioning and reviving aesthetics for the entire culture. Their own brand of poiesis is mirrored in Hillman's language describing it. Go to the margins to see the clear outline of things; see the clear reflection in what is rejected. Reflection in remembrance—seeing from a different window, through a different lens, hearing with different ears, being attuned to the beat of hip-hop, indigenous language, identity through style, fashion, creation, flipping a mass-produced Chevy or Nissan Altima into a stylized low-rider painted with a brilliant lacquer that makes the eyes tear up; displaying a gang's cryptic logo—all of this glistens when prodded into motion.

And then to ethics:

> Perhaps not your ethics, or mine, for ours tend to live in the modern divorce between duty and beauty. But in the gang and the hood and the street, there is a code of honor, of truth telling like it is, of heightened sensitivity to insult and dissing, and where attitudes of pretension are seen through.... The importance of shame, of dignity, of pride, of honor, loyalty, neighborhood, and family—. (199)

I mentioned above Hillman's own poetic aesthetic as a way into discussing beauty and ethics. Ugliness may at times be the *via regia* into such a topic. For assistance on the ugly he returns to Plotinus and his *Enneads*: "*kakon aischrotes*, which also means evil, bad, turpitude, shameful, obscene: An ugly thing is something that has not been entirely mastered by form *(morphos)*" (204). Our response to it is to recoil, to cringe, and to put distance from it. But when the ugly can no longer be distinguished from the beautiful, when what once repelled us is now numbly accepted, then something of the ethical sense of things, actions, ideas and governances takes a beating and winds up in intensive care. A valued quality of our being is insulted, wounded and the affliction remains, often with no medical coverage; one is out of the system.

I sense here the development of a mass conformity because the practice of discernment itself sits in the back of the cinder block classroom, unobserved and indifferent to what is taking place in the front of the room. Do so many not vote or otherwise engage in any communal events or allow their voices to be heard because they have lost the sense of aesthetics? Seems like a troubling stretch. But that is what Hillman wants us to feel: it is far-fetched and true, true because seemingly so far-fetched. Like a poet, James is unafraid, in fact yearns for, those interstices where the distorted brings delight, the torqued troubles and the gnarled, well, is allowed to twist and shout.

Works Cited

Giroux, Henry A. *The Violence of Organized Forgetting: Thinking Beyond America's Disimagination Machine.* San Francisco: City Light Books, 2014.

Hillman, James. *City and Soul.* Edited Robert Leaver, Preface Gail Thomas. Vol. 2. *Uniform Edition of the Writings of James Hillman.* Putnam, Connecticut: Spring Publications, 2006.

Hillman, James and Sonu Shamdasani. *Lament of the Dead: Psychology After Jung's* Red Book. New York: Norton, 2013.

II

CULTURAL ESSAYS

CHAPTER 11

THE TERRIBLE COST OF TRUST

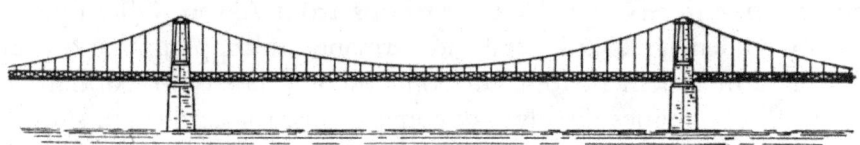

From 9/11 to 4/11 seems like an eternal gap; then again, it was just yesterday. How to say anything about it has been part of my dilemma; yet to say it, to give it language to fix it in a ceremony of speech, is a necessity. Something at the heart of our national psyche seeks to be remembered; such a recollection makes it part of our national identity.

The passenger planes on 11 September crashed into and penetrated a zone that had been prepared for by one of our own, Timothy McVeigh who opened a canister of terrorism with his bombing of the Oklahoma City Federal building that can never be closed. The best we can do is acknowledge it, reflect on it, come home to it, a kind of *nostos* of the imagination—without trying to solve it or deflect its lasting import. I hope if we do nothing else today, we don't move to solve terrorism, for I am not certain we even have a handle on violence in all its mutations both personal and collective. Nor have we found it useful or important to explore the mythologies, both personal and collective, that guide the missiles of terrorist acts around the globe.

I thus enter this brief reflection with you by finding a toehold, a place from which to grasp the terror of terrorism and to ask what terrorism feeds on, what it fuels itself with, what its energy source is? There are many untapped avenues to be explored in order to try to apprehend the symptoms of terrorism as a solution, an insoluble solution. When I sat on the edge of our bed at home in Goleta, California after my wife called me from the bedroom early that morning to see one of the New York towers burning, I saw from the right corner of the television screen another plane flying towards the towers, probably doing reconnaissance viewing, I thought. Then it too disappeared, and for a brief instant, nothing; then the invisible plane transformed into a fireball that pushed out of the other side of the second tower. Instantly I felt the same shock and numbness begin in my legs and creep up to my shoulders as I did 32 years ago when I arrived on the campus of Kent State University campus a short time after National Guard troops from Akron, Ohio opened fire on students, killing several and permanently crippling four others.

The first element to assault one: incomprehension. All barriers drop, all boundaries dissolve, all conventions, for an instant, suffer a hiatus. Something beyond the human order, yet contained within it, enters what was a moment ago safe habitable space: a university campus, the work place of commerce, an ancient street of Jerusalem within hand grenade throwing distance to the Holy of Holies. What evaporates in these spaces is one of the qualities on which civilization rests, an order is somewhat assured and a cosmos maintains its integrity: TRUST.

In the aftermath of 11 September and in the current throes of terrorist suffering in the Middle East, I am forced to consider the deep place that Trust plays in the maintenance and sustained existence of a civilized space. Trust is the central fabric of what has been called the "sensus communis," or a common sense and a shared sensibility that over time, one simply assumes. Pull that rug out from under people and what is left? Something simple creeps in here: when a traffic light gives me a green to go, I trust others will stop; the food I purchase I trust will not harm me or my family; I must trust the propane canister's relation to our BBQ grill that when I ignite it to cook a meal, it will not blow up in my face; when I mail a letter to our sons in another city, I trust the postal system to deliver it in a reasonable time frame. These matters are so unconscious, so casual, so taken for granted that their rupture or absence is in proportion to their presence. Trust, I would say, is mythic because it is what holds a people together; it entrusts something to each of us, one another and a shared or communal sense of a common good.

I believe there is an imagination of Trust, an imagination that learns to Trust. From the beginning of a child's life, her development is tightly coiled around Trust. In its absence, what rushes in to replace it? Suspicion, fear, hate, resentment, self-protection and self-interest enter and grow out of all proportion. Having one's person violated, invaded, or one's property seized by force or stealth are such heinous crimes because they violate Trust that is at the heart of human freedom. Fear, perhaps the greatest infection in Trust's absence, is invited in to replace it. Without Trust, freedom shrinks, becomes impotent, less operative, less a felt sense in the sensus communis, the communal order which gains in its power and stature because of the mythic elements that sustain it. Trust sustains the common good; distrust oxidizes that same good.

All of us know and have felt what a profound change occurs in our relation with another, with a place of employment, with a place of worship, when Trust can no longer be imagined because it has been dislodged and violated. Then, the myth of Trust, as a fabric covering or embracing different, disparate but nonetheless unified elements, is torn, tattered. Trust is a bedrock to any growth, development, or bonding of love and desire. Pull out Trust from beneath the stand of an individual or a people and there is little left to build on. Suspicion, like a worm burrowing into the crisp white meat of an apple, destroys it from the inside out.

Our rush to reestablish Trust, desperately to replace or develop a pale simulacrum of its organic and flexible quality in synthetic form, is now being futilely constructed around us, like a chrysalis that is faulty and frail. Like a bogus insurance policy, it is fraught with so many clauses, conditions and disclaimers that it appears more like an apology than an integral rebuilding of Trust. I speak now for a moment about Security. We have even named a Security Czar, and how we seem to love the sound of that exotic Russian epithet out of a dynasty that has long passed.

Security measures are a brutal and often futile witness to Trust's erosion and to an organic quality of Trust that legislation or scanners cannot replace. Security measures—searches, ethnic and racial profiling, interrogations, air marshals, locked, bolted, barred bullet-proof fire doors—are thin and finally vulnerable failures that seek to replace the organic, ontological and individually-espoused Trust with a clanking mechanism of security measures. Terrorism is a physical act of destruction and an ontological force of annihilation; it evaporates freedom, the freedom to imagine even as it foments a failed familial infrastructure.

Trust, in its compassionate base, offers security as a by-product. Now, however, the by-product is quickly becoming the staple. Ultimately however, it is impossible to deploy security measures from without as a consciously-built form of Trust that must and does develop from within. Trust is a virtue—security is its pale shadow, a simulacrum. It is uneven and outward-seeking. Trust is unself-conscious; security is totally, even hyper-conscious. Trust rests on concern for the other; security rests on concern for itself. Trust is almost intangible in its growth, even its presence, but tangible in its effects; security is only tangible outwardly. Trust is an interior movement of the soul in love; security is an exterior motion of a system demanding uncanny outpourings of labor.

If I cannot trust you or you cannot trust me, then we have no ground beneath our feet to stand and face one another, if not in love, than in mutual respect. Love itself establishes Trust as fertile soil in which to grow, from which to draw nourishment. What is more painful to the vulnerable ears of another: "I no longer love you"? or "I no longer trust you"? Something of Trust's nature goes to the ontological core of our being. Nowhere does there exist an insurance policy to protect us from Trust's absence, even though an entire industry, perhaps the biggest in this country, rests on a wager between Trust and its absence.

What happens to a people when Trust is eroded?—and we see how fragile and ephemeral it can be. Fear, anxiety, loss of freedom all conspire in Trust's absence or sadly injured presence. Such, for me, is the terr-ible energy of Terrorism. It opens and secures each of our vulnerabilities to what is untrue, self-serving and divorced from a larger whole.

CHAPTER 12

SCIENCE, MATH—AND MYTH. WHY NOT?

I am a mythologist who snuck in the back door of this field through literature and depth psychology. With degrees in literature and psychology from three schools, I fell in love with stories from the get-go but knew there was something lurking beneath the plots that I wasn't getting to, much less registering with. Fairy tales fascinated me as a child. I would find ways to fake the flu so that I could stay in bed, knowing that my mother, an avid reader, would go to the public library and pick out 8-10 books for me to read. In bed, I would burrow under the covers with a flashlight and my little plastic clock radio; there in my own crib I would read while listening to Nat King Cole, the Maguire Sisters, Sinatra and dream the day or days away. Eventually pushed out of my lair, I trudged back to Holy Cross Elementary school, the good Ursuline Sisters and boring lessons.

But in 1988 I, with millions of others, watched hypnotically the PBS series of interviews with Bill Moyers and Joseph Campbell all recorded at George Lucas' Skywalker Ranch in California. In this series, *The Power of Myth*, of animated conversations, peppered with mythic images and stories, we as a nation learned the extent to which the purpose, the power and the privilege a people's mythology has on their sense of values, justice, laws, customs, remembrances through rituals as popular as the recent Super Bowl contest or the World Series in baseball. Even the terms "super" and "world" call up something mythic in our collective imagination.

In the series of talks, Joseph Campbell, whose 100th anniversary of his birth was March 26th 2004, blueprinted for us the important presence of a people's mythology. Unfortunately, he died of cancer before the series aired. Campbell believed that myths served as organizing principles for both individuals, tribes, cultures, even as vast as entire civilizations. Knowing one's myth was as important in his mind as knowing one's name, one's ancestry, one's blood type; it gave one a context in a world that often left one feeling place-less and orphaned from a larger profound whole. In response to Moyers' query on the kinds of questions asked by our ancestors about life, Campbell responds: "There is a basic mythological motif that originally all was one, and then there was separation—heaven and earth, male and female, and so forth. How did we lose touch with the unity?" (*Power* 53).

In *The Hero's Journey* he further stresses the point that having and knowing one's personal mythos grounds one, centers one in place so that the individual is not buffeted about by the latest fad or belief that swirls around him or her. Myths, then are grounding and stabilizing for the individual psyche. To be truly alive and vital, he wrote in *Flight of the Wild Gander*, myths must offer in pictorial form cosmogonic and ontological intuitions: "They are not to be judged as true or false, but as effective or ineffective, maturative or pathogenic. They are rather like enzymes, products of the body in which they work; . . . and employed as catalysts of spiritual (i.e., psychological) well-being" (*Flight* xiv). Note that for Campbell in his drawing an analogy between the body and mythology, there is an intimate cross-pollinating of mythos with bios.

Today, as I continue to teach a course on several of Joseph Campbell's major works to my adult students, I recognize more fully how hungry are we individually and as a nation for mythic—not fast or frozen—nourishment. We are indeed a nation overweight and underfed; myth has been erased from the pyramid of essential food groups, and the absence is becoming more pronounced and devastating. To suffer from the disease of "mythic dissociation," he writes, is "where the sense of the sacred is still officially dissociated from this earth and its life" *(Flight* 186), is to feel a profound divorce from life, from nature and from the world. Witness the tremendous success of the recent *Harry Potter* films, or *Whale Rider*, or the spectacular success of *The Lord of the Rings* trilogy. Reflect back for a moment to the *Star Wars* series, which George Lucas credited Joseph Campbell's work with inspiring and helping him to organize, create and bring to fruition on the popular screen, where many forms of the hero interact. Even *Finding Nemo* carries a large mythic freight underwater.

All myths, Campbell believes, are metaphors for actions and events in our interior life that can assist us to become more aware of our life's meaning. *Follow Your Bliss* reached bumper sticker status. But he was no sentimentalist; he believed following one's bliss created its own unique assortment of blisters. Journeying towards one's destiny is not a stroll in the park. And many of those blisters earned on the way are long lasting, slow to heal, and leave palpable scars on body and soul. Furthermore, his heroes when he was a young boy were Buffalo Bill Cody and Native American plains Indians, Leonardo daVinci; in his college years, James Joyce, Oswald Spengler, Arthur Schopenhauer, Heinrich Zimmer and Friederich Nietzsche peopled his mature influences. His writings helped immeasurably in dismantling a false dichotomy between myth (a lie!) and fact (a truth!). Myths, he believed, revealed a deeper style of truth not available to fact. "Mythology," he quipped in *Flight of the Wild Gander*, "is misread then as direct history or science, symbols become fact, metaphor dogma, and the quarrels of the sects arise, each mistaking its own symbolic signs for ultimate reality…" *(Flight* 53).

So my own desire takes hold here: in addition to science and math requirements, which exercise intellect and reason, I propose a basic course or two on mythology using Campbell's work as a primer. Better. Offer it as an elective on the secondary level. If the hunger for myth is anything like my adult students', who feel deeply nourished by them, then there will be no shortage of students signing up. Studying mythology, reading myths like Narcissus and Echo, Psyche and Eros, Demeter and Persephone, taps deeper dimensions of my students' lives. That they have raised families, changed careers, suffered deaths of loved ones, wondered what their lives were adding up to and what direction they were heading in—all this becomes rich material that myths evoke and ask us to ponder from an imaginal, or what I call mytho-poetic, rather than a rational, point of view. I have learned that people need to be educated by stories as much, if not more, than by facts and information. Part of this phenomenon, I suspect, is that psyche is fundamentally poetic, analogic, metaphoric and symbolic in its movement.

Joseph Campbell is a national treasure; yet he is still underrated, maligned by many academics as un-scholarly, seen as prejudiced, too opinionated, and generally not one of the boys. Like his own definition of the hero, he broke from tradition, entered the forest alone, following his own bliss, and returned with the boon of world mythologies to enrich all people. A national holiday? Too much. National recognition in this centenary year of his birth? Way overdue.

Joseph Campbell: may the force continue to be with you and with all who take up your books and recordings to further their own, ferociously unique, mythic pilgrimage. A nation's people, ceasing to venture inward with a mythical sensibility, are open to any form of warped thought, propaganda and self-absorbed political, theological and mass-media *poshlust*.

CHAPTER 13

HOLY TERROR: THE WHITE WHALE
AND THE AMERICAL MYTHOS

The language that couches the response to Terrorism, whether in its real or imagined threats, needs its own capital letter now. Yet that same language continues to grow more and more anemic and flat as we witness another wave of assaults on a major city capital. "Freedom is on the march," "Stay the course," "We are winning the war on Terror," "The insurgents are collapsing." Yet the prognosis, if we consider soberly a front page article in the *Santa Barbara News Press* Sunday, 10 July [2006]: "Experts paint grim picture of 'endless war' against terrorism" is far less benign.

The language flattens into empty mantras of hope that seem to bear less resemblance to the reality unfolding on the world scene. Terrorism, however, has become the new window frame through which we look out on the world from a promised bunker of "Security" and "Safety," more language that is often belied by the facts of these measures. Such is the new format of communication for people who have and continue to imagine the United States, and indeed the West, as predatory, bullying, consuming barbarians whose time has come to be stopped or at least dismantled through its own obsession with capitalism. Is it worth, then, changing the way one is able to imagine the constantly rising toll in fighting enemies we cannot see, who seem to emerge from the depths, strike and then evaporate in a vapor? The number of their minions seem to be growing and limitless in their population.

I have spent a large measure of my life studying literary classics. One of my favorites that I continue to teach each year is Herman Melville's eloquent masterpiece, *Moby-Dick* published in 1851. I see in its finer political lineaments as I work on board the Pequod to fathom with my students, as best I can, the genius of Melville's vision of, among other pockets of western culture, the face of democracy. His epic novel is as much a political tract that, if heeded, would change the course of the Terrorism conversation overnight, first of all, by tracking the way monomania looks when transformed into whaling policy aboard the Pequod, named after a Native American term meaning "Destroyer," or when same monomania couched in the soul of the enigmatic and deeply wounded Captain Ahab, morphs into public policy. Any separation from religion and politics grows ever thinner on the world stage and here at home.

More than one writer has suggested that the initials of the grand phantom of the white whale, MD, represents "Manifest Destiny," that sense bequeathed to a people believed to be "chosen," whose task, since ordained and delineated by God, is to lather its message of democracy across the globe. Okay. For me, however, MD could just as easily stand for "Manic-Depressive," "Maniacal-Design," "Misdirected-Deployment," or, in a more cynical vein, Manifest-Deviance." Even weapons of (M)ass-(D)estruction does not seem a far stretch, for from the novel's point of view, such is the case when the Pequod, down to the last splinter of her quarter deck, is sunk by the swirling mass created by the wounded white leviathan.

What is the story of *Moby-Dick* in its broadest cloth? It relates an adventure, from the point of view of one depressed orphan at the time of his initial voyage, and whose name, Ishmael, recalls his Old Testament prototype, son of Hagar, orphaned and abandoned in the Middle East. The modern-day figure survives the destruction of his whale ship to tell the story and to inspire a more communal understanding that "we are all spliced together," and that all mortals' lifelines are globally entangled in a grand community, in what one psychological figure of thought calls the "unus mundus." He recounts the story of one Captain Ahab who, in hunting whales, came upon and did battle with a white sperm whale, the very one who "dismasted him" of one of his legs in an earlier combat when it turned on the hunter and transformed the aggressor into helpless prey. Full of revenge of the fury of insult and believing that the white whale was either the agent or principle of unchecked evil in the world—we might translate it as *axis of evil* in the modern lexicon—Ahab placed his entire ship of state in jeopardy by designing a single-minded quest to assassinate what he perceived and successfully seduced his crew into believing was the origin of evil itself. Such is his interpretation of the watery beast from his wounded and vengeful angle of vision. Ask another crew member and one receives other possibilities as to the nature of this watery wonder.

Now, as the whaling industry is actually a whale oil industry, the purpose of whaling was to hunt, boil and barrel as much oil as one could before heading back, in this case, to capital-rich New Bedford. But this whaling voyage on board the Pequod has only one purpose outlined and insisted upon by its captain: to find and slay the white whale as either agent or principle of evil incarnate. It finally makes little difference as to its true nature; for Ahab the distinction is a moot point. Yet on another deeper level, it is the story of American democracy, as Melville hints at in more than one place in the epic. Recall for a moment these lines from the chapter entitled "Knights and Squires": "men may seem detestable as joint stock-companies and nations: knaves, fools and murderers there may be.... But, man, in the ideal, is so noble and so sparkling, such a grand and glowing creature, that over any ignominious blemish in him all his fellows should run to throw their costliest robes" (123). He goes on to praise the inherent dignity of man, in which one can discern in the worker who "wields a pick or drives a spike; that democratic dignity which... radiates without end from God; Himself! The great God absolute! The centre and circumference of all democracy! His omnipresence, our divine equality!" (123). What a lyric pronouncement of the quality and value of the individual, a sustained centerpiece of freedom and dignity prescribed in the American mythos. Sounds like an encomium to the Middle Class of America, acknowledging the millions who toil daily to promote, in part, the sustained dignity of the American enterprise. Yet, one overzealous commander can turn the entire project into a whirling heap of wooden splinters.

Behind such praise, however, prowls a shadow of the myth no less powerful and darkly radiant. Retribution, vengeance, woundedness, unyielding predatory self-righteousness, all expressed most poignantly in an almost cult-like rhetoric by the Captain to follow his maniacal lead as he gathers the entire crew on the quarter deck. There he offers his defense for going to war with Nature, then drives a gold doubloon into the main mast as economic gain for him who first spots the white whale, and demands non-negotiable fidelity to his mission: to eradicate what he has decided is the source of evil incarnate. All, even lowly and wise Ishmael, succumb to the Captain's persuasive demands of unconditional and unquestioned patriotism. Only the first mate, Starbuck, is courageous enough to question the captain's designs; but he is quickly sidelined as a voice without consequence and is effectively silenced.

Yet no credible explanation or proof from the dismembered Captain is forthcoming to prove or support his wild claim that the white whale is evil's agency, much less its principle, all on board simply accept it as fact, so powerfully and persuasively has Ahab's paternal and iron-clad media-blitz on board successfully framed the hunt as well as the final sticking point of its harpoons; weapons of mass whale destruction. No amount of casualties or even humanitarian pleas from other whale boat captains for assistance can dissuade Ahab from his singular course of action: to slay in vengeance through the prism of a self-righteous woundedness that terrifies, one which seems to give his life a purpose it did not possess until that instant of fierce and indifferent dismemberment.

Such are the two broad bands of the American myth wherein public commerce becomes so entangled with private mania that leads, as we remember, to the sinking of the Pequod by that "ungraspable phantom of life," the white whale. It is no accident that the Pequod's crew members include individuals from around the globe. How thick and rich, like the mystical substance from the whale's head, ambergris itself, even mythic could be the discussion on our world predicament if only those who wield language's brittle metaphors were open to such a discussion with often disastrous effects, untold pain and loss, and rapacious addiction to power. Yet, in the powerful and so limited Fear Frame that the present conversation is installed within, I am made to feel like one of those whalers on the quarter deck being told: "conform to my vision."

Freedom, in such suffocating circumstances, seems as deep and fathomless and out of reach as the white whale itself. Yes, Melville's masterpiece is still read, but it remains largely, like the voice of the first mate, Starbuck, still unheeded.

CHAPTER 14

LUCY UNDER GLASS

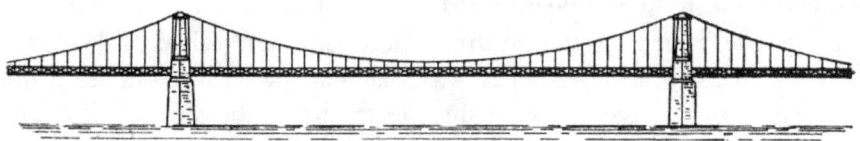

When my wife and I read an article by Blake Edgar in the November/December issue of *Archaeology* magazine that the oldest hominid yet discovered, Lucy, named by her discoverer, Dr. Don Johanson in the 1970s, was exhibited at the Houston Museum of Natural Science, we decided that seeing "the world's most famous fossil" was not to be missed. Fossils are fascinating dehydrated facts in another form; yet they carry the residue of history like no other species. Witnessing them offers a built-in perspective of our place in the scheme of things. So we packed the truck and headed east to Houston.

We made reservations for the Friday morning after Thanksgiving to enter the exhibit and to view the *original* remains of this tiny woman who lived 3.2 million years ago in an area of Ethiopia. Two impulses drew us: our own abiding interest in ancestry as well as a rare opportunity to see not a replica—which is what folks view even when they visit the museum in Ethiopia—but her abiding original person that would peer out at us through a glass case in the main exhibit room.

We were drawn to her as we might be drawn to the remains of

Eve, ribbed from Adam in the story of *Genesis*. Moreover, we could not fathom a human being living 3.2 million years ahead of us, so even to view her fossilized bones, leathery skin and still intact finger nails, would be to pull back for a few precious moments the curtain that separates us from such a distant corridor into our own heritage. We would in effect see our own faces through the temporal-spatial mirror of her fossilized form.

In a videotape that is part of the Houston exhibit running through April, 2008, Johanson describes where and how he discovered her. One more psychologically-minded might also evidence another point of view: Lucy was ready to be found. He describes how, after exploring the slope of a mountain all day, he and his aides were heading back to camp when "I glanced over my shoulder at something that the sun had illuminated" and stopped. He walked back to see amid the dirt of the slope a shard of bone—an elbow?—and then looked up the slope to see ribs, pelvis, and parts of a skull, all exposed. His belief was that had he missed this sighting, the rains could have easily washed Lucy down the slope and over a near-by ledge, losing her for all time under a pile of ancient, even prehistoric, debris. But he saw her and we have her—not the oldest hominid fossil but unarguably the most complete, especially her hip cavity, which links her in structure more to us than to apes because it reveals most emphatically the posture in which she walked upright.

So what will you see if you visit this exquisite exhibit, full of artifacts from Ethiopia, including icon-like paintings from recent history? As you peer over a glass case in a room suffused with subdued lighting, you will view: parts of one leg, a tibia, the ilium, the largest bone of her pelvis, a femur, which suggests in shape that she walked upright, all of her 60 pounds and 3.5 feet in height; a humerus, a scapula, with a shoulder blade joint; 7-8 vertebrae of various sizes; a third molar and several canine teeth. I asked the Docent if she had been tested for any DNA residue and he replied yes and no, archeoanthropologists had found none, but that Carbon-14 dating was fairly accurate as to her age. Finally, cranial fragments, five in number. Another *A. afarensis* skull, found in 2002, writes Edgar, coauthor of *From Lucy to Language,* will reveal what Lucy's facial features looked like. It will be very exciting to see her gazing back at us over scores of millennia. Next to her physical presence is a vertical model of exactly the same pieces in the glass case to reveal how she would have appeared standing up.

The above writing focused on the history and physiology of Lucy. But some deeper concerns stirred in us as we gazed through the looking glass of history; we had to ask ourselves what affect does seeing her have on the imagination of the viewer? I can speak only for myself, but considering the waves of people already there viewing her on the Friday morning we attended, something more than curiosity compelled those present to make this figure a center piece of their own lives for a brief historical moment.

First of all, to think of our species as being the age of Lucy, and perhaps earlier on our planet, incites proud feelings of our durability as a life form, especially as we live more fully into a tension that recognizes that we may be more rapidly exhausting the earth and our place on it than anyone has fully, much less accurately, calculated. Lucy also takes us both *back and down*, down into the psyche of us as a species, yes, but also down into the depths of our being and further, into questions of purpose and value. Lucy also instills in me moments of reflection: on one's own life, on one's destiny, on one's connection over chasms of time, to an intelligence that lived in such a way and perhaps with a primitive wisdom so as to make *us* even possible. She also makes me wonder if we today will possess the same wisdom to pass what remains of our own planetary reality down to others. The question cannot be answered without a serious reality check on our own behavior and on the condition of exhaustion that seems to be more prominent in our planet today.

To look, for example, at her teeth still embedded in her lower jaw bone; to see fingers that curved and had the capacity to hold and to carry things, since she walked upright and thus enjoyed a freedom to carry items; to see her pelvis and rib cage so similar to our own, though in miniature, is to see ourselves through the mirror of history in a timeline that is staggering to contemplate, fun to imagine and humbling to recollect. Lucy's presence in her original state stimulates our historical imagination to wonder, to ponder who and what we are as a species and to meditate on our own destiny, as Lucy may have indeed thought of her own, as well, perhaps, of her own family of origin, and of what the forests and deserts of her wanderings might promise and portend. What might have been her thoughts and feelings as she walked in search of certain plants to prepare, certain dangers to be ever vigilant towards?

This exhibit represents the first public display of Lucy in 3.2 million years. That fact alone was enough to drive us east from New Braunfels, Texas to view her, as did our younger son and several friends who met us at the museum; they too felt the draw eastward, to Houston, then east and south to Africa, to a plain where trees, mountain slopes and vegetation may have been the wellspring of all of us, then east to the beginnings of the planet, the origin of all life.

Lucy, it is not hard to imagine, is mother, matriarch and crone walking and feeling and hoping for a life that is so close to the origin of us all. Seeking after origins is one of the most mythic impulses imbedded in the consciousness of our communal longing. For that instinct alone, it was worth the pilgrimage to Houston to peer for a few moments, through the glass of history to a more primal and animated past at a sweet leathery face that held in its visage the entire race of humanity. No text could have brought us home with such tender power as did she.

CHAPTER 15

THE CONFLUENCE OF REMEMBERING AND FORGETTING

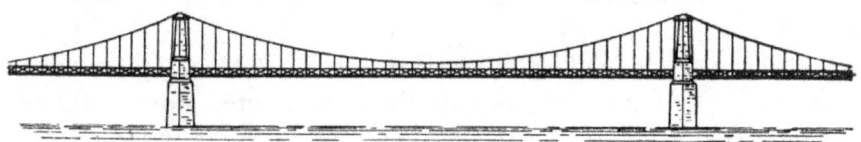

> However, the most powerfully effective of all the
> images and similes of forgetting comes down from
> myth, and in fact from the time of early Greek writers
> such as Hesiod and Pindar.
> ~Harald Weinrich, *Lethe: The Art and Critique of
> Forgetting* 6

I have successfully avoided both high school and college reunions. They always felt depressing. I envisioned myself standing around looking into faces I no longer knew, chatting with wives of those I no longer recognized and growing more despondent with each vignette conjured up to edify and enlighten who might be unlucky enough to be pulled into the vortex of nostalgia.

But when I received a notification for our 50th high school reunion as St. Joseph Viking graduates in Cleveland, Ohio, I thought: Ok, attend one, most likely the grand finale to a string of reunions I had sidestepped for decades. So I went and joined the troupe of others in June, 2013. I even served on the Planning Committee whose task it was to attempt to contact as many of the 300 Vikings I had graduated with in this all-male school managed by the Marianist Order of the Catholic Church.

For my date I brought one of my younger brothers, Bob, who had graduated two years after us in 1965; he was more than eager to attend and made a very relaxed companion for the evening.

The entire experience was memorable and, in moments, a joy. As I began to listen to individuals tell stories about others, I realized that a benefit lurked in this ritual: namely, that we would remember and so complete in small measure the lives of others in those young years between ages 15-18. Much was remembered and of course much more was forgotten. Remembering and forgetting made a suitable couple for the two day venture; we moved between these two moments of consciousness and in the journey crafted parts of our lives back into a more cohesive and coherent story than the one we entered with. That in itself was worth the price of the pilgrimage from Texas to Ohio.

In Homer's epic, *The Odyssey,* Helen, wife of Menelaos, now back from Troy, gives those listening to the remembered stories of Troy's violent war a drug to help them forget. Nepenthe is the drug and it soothes the sufferings of those who were asked to remember through narratives of the action (Book IV). Before arriving home from his ten year sojourn from Troy to Ithaca, Odysseus experiences a seven year isolation on the island of the goddess Calypso; there, daily sitting alone at the edge of a promontory looking out to sea, the warrior/voyager gestates in memories of home, his beloved wife, Penelope and their son Telemachos he may have not yet seen.

Before this time he journeys to many lands to confront a wide range of images of the home with his ever-decreasing number of survivors of Troy; one of these locales is the land of the Lotus-Eaters, who try to persuade him and his warriors to eat of the Lotus flower and so forget home, if not, indeed, the entirety of their histories. Later the goddess Circe, who with magical powers transforms all of Odysseus' men to swine but who in their transformation retain their human minds, gives them all a potion that makes them forget. Other incidents could be named; the epic creates a continuous zigzagging patterned journey between remembering and forgetting. Back in Ithaca, becoming too attached to their appetites makes the suitors of Penelope forget the values inherent in the fundamental guest-host relationship that undergirds Greek civilization's right order and social measure.

Dante's 14th century *Commedia* is also in large degree a skirmish between remembering and forgetting. He cannot remember, and confesses as much, in writing the poem, certain feelings or events and asks us as readers to fill in the blanks with our own narrative insights. In *Paradiso*, forgetting accelerates to such a degree that the poet must discard much from the poem in order to realize an intact vision in his epic's last cantos.

In the 18th century, Rousseau's *Confessions* also depicts the struggle between memory and forgetting. He tells us early on that he promises to remember accurately, but the farther back he goes in his own history, the more he is sure he will forget, so he may have to default to embellishing his narrative in order to keep it intact and coherent (*Confessions* 2). Toni Morrison's more recent award-winning epic novel, *Beloved,* develops the character of a former slave woman, Sethe, who, after trying to murder all her children to liberate them from a life of slavery, but succeeds in killing only one of them, reaches a state of mind of attempting to remember nothing. Her name, Sethe, Morrison commented, was the closest she could find to rhyme with Lethe, which in Greek mythology is the river of forgetfulness that flows throughout the underworld. Instead, her dead daughter, known only as Beloved, reappears in order to haunt her mother and to force her to remember her slain child after the latter's throat was sliced with a hand saw in the shed behind 124 Bluestone Road 18 years earlier. At novel's end, Beloved, or whatever it has metamorphosed into, flees from the house and disappears; all agree that she was not a story to remember, so the entire community disremembers her.

In Aldous Huxley's *Brave New World,* the Controller of Conditioning, Mustafa Mund, understands as a matter of pride the necessity of eliminating history. He follows the mantra of the ruling god of the age, Henry Ford, whose observation, "History is bunk," guides the imagination of the new world order. Mund's goal is to whisk from the communal memory the writings of Plato, Aristotle, Dante, Shakespeare—indeed all the classics of humanities education because they distract the mind from its number one occupation: consuming in a perennial state of engineered diversions. "Whisk, Whisk—and where was Odysseus, where was Job, where were Jupiter and Gotama and Jesus? Whisk—and those specks of antique dirt called Athens and Rome?" (41). He also is fully aware that a people unable to sustain a memory are most easily manipulated by whatever is placed in front of them in the moment. Huxley outlines the beginnings of Attention Deficit Disorder that leaves a people without a ground in place or time.

Linda Hogan's fine contemporary novel, *Solar Storms,* has a character describe how she cut her hair that grew a certain length during the time a particularly unpleasant person stayed with her. By cutting her hair back to the length it was before her house guest arrived, she found it easier to forget her and the painful experiences that occurred during her visit.

Finally, I mention the immortal short story, "Funes the Memorius" by the Argentine writer, Jorge Luis Borges. Borges describes a young man he met while visiting a small village in Argentina. He saw him only three times, the last in 1887. Ireneo Funes, the subject of the short story, while riding a half-tamed horse one day, was thrown off and paralyzed in the accident. From that day forward he was confined to a cot, which was often placed by his bedroom window so he could entertain himself by gazing down into the street. One evening Borges visits him in the back of his house. He soon learns that Funes has become capable of retaining everything he sees, reads or thinks. He has at the same time because of this uncanny ability, become incapable of forgetting anything. For all of his feats of learning, for instance, English, French, Portuguese and Latin, he was "incapable of thought. To think is to forget differences, generalize, make abstractions. In the teeming world of Funes, there were only details, almost immediate in their presence" ("Funes" 154).

Borges suggests, and subsequent studies have borne him out, that forgetting is as important to our sense of identity as remembering; we must be able to do so if we are to live a full and joyful life. We seem to be defined as much by what we disremember as by what we sustain and maintain of our experiences, beliefs and thoughts.

At the end of his superior study of forgetting cited earlier, Weinrich concludes his book with a chapter entitled "Stored, in Other Words, Forgotten." There he offers the following observation that all of us will have no difficulty relating to:

It has become evident that we now live in a society that has access to too much information, in which genuine skill in conducting one's life consists not in gathering information—these days any child can do that on the Internet—but in knowing how to reject information—and for this the Internet still offers no program. (208)

What he calls us to is a practice of "Annulment" whereby "Documents are put into the shredder rather than into file cabinets" (209). Only some 2% of all material is archived. We then become not hoarders of information but "thrower-aways" that delight in pitching information, documents, records and bytes of information as an act of independence. One has to wonder if we store data for later retrieval that may never happen on the grounds that we have the technical capacity to do so. However, there is some truth to the effect that we each must forget certain things in order to remember anything. Might television shows like "Hoarders" be cultural expressions of shared symptoms that guide us to a larger cultural malady of our inability to let go of what is unnecessary based on our inability to discern what is important from what is worthy of a journey to the shredder?

To move this discussion one step further: the cultural critic Avishai Margalit suggests in his study, *The Ethics of Memory*, that we may have to develop far beyond what we have reached thus far in deciding if we may have an ethical obligation to remember certain things *and* that we have a similar obligation to forget certain things. "Communities must make decisions and establish institutions that foster forgetting as much as remembering. Shredding the personal files of old Stasi (the former East German secret services) is an example of a communal decision to forget" (13). Margalit pushes off from an ethics of memory to pose the question: do we have a moral imperative to remember certain events while relegating others to the river Lethe?

Memories We Live By

What we carry memorially both within and without are fundamentally events transformed into stories, the vignettes that shape us, inform us and most crucially, form us. Personal memories and personal mythologies are of a piece. I sense that our personal and collective myths comprise the inner sleeve of history itself. The myth hidden in the sleeve's interior gives shape to the sleeve's outer form, what we can see and witness. Robert Armstrong calls hidden myth a "mythoform," a bedrock, founding, grounding energy that, he suggests, "is the generative principle of culture, both the substance of culture and a mode in which that substance is enacted and exists" (*Wellspring* 126).

C.G. Jung offers a concrete presence of this mythoform in his autobiography. When he asked himself what he thoroughly enjoyed doing as a young boy, he recalled how much he loved building things with stones. His fantasy world began to take shape through his building. So, late in life, he bought property and began to build with stones. He then offers us this reminiscence:

> Naturally, I thought about the significance of what I was doing, and asked myself, "Now, really, what are you about? You are building a small town, and doing it as if it were a rite!" I had no answer to my question, only the inner certainty that I was on the way to discovering my own myth. (qtd. in "Incipit," *Riting Myth, Mythic Writing*)

His words carry an oblique invitation to each of us to explore what rites we deploy to discover such an important element of ourselves, our personal myth. It grows out of an "inner certainty" that the path of exploration is true for us. When we remember we mythologize and imagine; when we imagine mythically we engage an act of remembrance, shrouded always within acts of forgetting. When we remember Michelangelo's observation on sculpting a block of marble, we discern in his image of this art form a marriage between remembering and forgetting. He believed that a figure was imprisoned within the marble he chose to sculpt; his task as sculptor-liberator was to chip away those parts of the block that impeded the figure's appearance; discarding them would yield the figure's presence by liberating it from captivity. I imagine his chipping away the parts of the stone as artistic acts of forgetting so that he might more keenly re-member the figure within. What emerges into the world is possible only by forgetting and remembering joining in a partnership to create a third thing—the imagined figure resting uneasily inside the block, patiently awaiting its birth into the world until the right liberator appears.

Joseph Campbell believes that the function of a mythology is to integrate one's conscious existence into one's unconscious life. When a mythology we are living in does not operate *on us*, it needs to be chipped away, forgotten, rejected and abandoned. One who lives in a myth is fascinated by an aspiration, Campbell continues. I would add that myths inspire as well; they offer us a quickening of consciousness and a glimpse into our destiny if we are able to listen closely to what it is the world speaks most poignantly to us: "Our outward-oriented consciousness, addressed to the demands of the day, may lose touch with these inward forces; and the myths, states Jung, when correctly read, are the means to bring us back in touch" (*Myths to Live By* 14). Myths, then, inspire us to aspire. Motion is at the heart of psyche's existence; to be in motion can signal that we are mythically driven, so long as we have entered our own pathless path and not someone else's.

Patterns of Retention; Patterns of Rejection

Jung reminds us further that psyche has within it patterns of organization that shape material over a lifetime. Psyche tends to pre-shape human experience and organize it in patterned ways. Patterns can be both personal and collective; they encompass shaping forces working on all material entering one's consciousness. My own sense is that they are also stylized to accommodate a particular manner of being. This line of thought leads me to believe how we remember and forget along patterns of purpose and meaning as well. We forget in patterned ways. With some reward, we each might reflect on our experiences both remembered and forgotten to distinguish any pattern in the content of our rememberings and forgettings.

For example, are there qualities of otherness, those that appear foreign or alien, that bring us to forget certain circumstances, situations and conditions? Given that remembering and forgetting are mythic functions of our narrative beings, might we gain insights into its formatting principles by attending to what we remember and forget? Recall for a moment how, in the last cantos of *Purgatorio* in

Dante's *Commedia,* and just prior to his pilgrimage to *Paradiso* with Beatrice as his guide, he must be submerged by Matilda, Beatrice's handmaiden, into the rivers of Lethe and Enoe, the rivers first of forgetfulness and then of remembrance (*Purgatorio* XXXIII. 85-145). Psychologically and emotionally he must be brought to a critical point of forgetting what has held his soul back as well as remembering what he has done well in order to move to the highest level of spiritual awakening. Surely there is an essential and necessary conspiracy between the two realms of consciousness that together myth-make and myth-shape our developing awareness.

We each may reach an understanding of our narrative's meaning according to its mythic structure, its underlying mythoform, to recall Armstrong's word. The mythoform:

- Makes the myth cohere
- Shapes the template I impose on it
- Embodies the beliefs I maintain to keep the narrative fixed, intact and coherent
- Forces that hold confusion at bay
- Deflects what does not fit
- Promises little or no distortion of the facts.

Narrative polish and narrative smoothing of the blunt edges are acts that can blur distinctions between events themselves and a more valuable discovery. So, my narrative parts are asked to fit the findings of the mythic structure that oversees them" (*Narrative Truth* 27) Donald Spence continues by observing that narrative truth has a special significance in its own right. Making connection with the actual past may be far less significant than creating a coherent and consistent account of a particular set of facts (28). We create this coherence and consistency by discovering the right and appropriate proportion between remembering and forgetting. We recollect the details of an historical event by adding and subtracting particulars in order to make a story more "truthful" and coherent, one that allows a deeper understanding of our narrative to assist self-coherence. If we can change the context of our remembering and forgetting, we may transform the terms of the story.

Narrative truth is a criterion we employ to decide when a certain experience has been captured to our satisfaction. It depends, of course, on continuity running to closure as well as the way the fit of the pieces takes on an aesthetic finality (40). Once a given construction acquires a narrative truth, it becomes just as real as any other kind of truth. Often it is the case that this new reality becomes a significant part of a deeper healing. The upshot of this creative process is that I must forget certain things in order to remember anything. My historical truth engages what has happened to me and in what fashion and disposition I remember those events. My narrative truth is the language I use to capture what has happened to me, in the poetic logic of a story that brings all pieces into a coherent whole. One then is forced to ask: what story or stories have I shaped out of this historical truth I have lived in and through? In any reading of a story, Spence insists, even if it is our own narrative recollected, or a story we have read, "we cannot help but read into the text our own assumptions about time, place, and intentions…" (51).

In working with the ideas above and wishing to ground them in one's own mythic narrative, I propose entering it through the following corridors:

- I can remember what I believe
- I can believe what I remember
- I can remember what I have been taught to believe
- I too often believe what I remember "as-if" it were valid
- I remember what holds me/contains me/maintains me
- With a slight turn I remember what can suddenly transform me
- I can work to forget what habitual forms of thought incarcerate me
- Certain events and incidents I must continually remember to forget
- I may hold on to beliefs through which what I remember continues to wound me/sour me/curdle me
- Beliefs, ideas and recollections about myself and others comprise the filters, the patterned structures and the contexts by which I re-collect myself into the future
- I have the capacity to grieve my way to liberation
- Grieving allows me to return to the present and live there
- Frees me to live as an adult

- I continually ask myself: what habits of thought do I wish to remember and cultivate today and which to starve by forgetting?
- The above decisions will influence and sculpt my quality of life and the contextual terms of my narrative truth

The Quest to Forget

Mircea Eliade writes a formidable essay on "Mythologies of Memory and Forgetting." In it he reminds us that "The fountain Lethe, 'forgetfulness,' is a necessary part of the realm of Death. The dead are those who have lost their memories" (71). We don't take this insight too literally, but rather in the spirit which I have attempted to convey above, there is as part of forgetting an insistence that parts of our past enter Hades as a consequence of our forgetting them, allowing at the same time for other remembrances to inhabit our interior landscape.

Marianne Lamers points out in a fine article, "The Importance of Forgetting," that remembering can occur only if we also forget (28). She offers the rich metaphor of a giant rain forest; there things are constantly dying off and proliferating, so that the health of the rain forest is predicated on much that is to be forgotten, sloughed off and encouraged to seep into the earth. It falls back into the rich loam of the forest floor and fertilizes new remembrances (29). She outlines her work, abbreviated as EMDR (eye movement desensitization and reprocessing) which helps memories find their right home in our organic structure so that traumatic experiences, which may not have been stored correctly and consequently wander throughout the brain, may find their rightful home (30).

Karl Kereny's mythically-inflected essay, "Mnemosyne— Lesmosyne," reveals the river Lethe as a domain of hiddenness, both of oneself as well as what one wants to avoid, not notice what is hidden. Suffering the wounds of remembrance has an escape clause: forgetfulness (121). He compares both remembering and forgetting by observing: "Just as Lethe is the spring which is drunk and flows through, so accordingly Mnemosyne can originally have been that which springs forth" (127). He goes on to inform us that "'Lesmosyne' derives from the same root as "Lethe' and means exactly the same thing.... Lethe makes everything disappear that belongs to the dark side of human existence" (129-30). What is most illuminating is that a complete portrait of the Goddess Mnemosyne is possible only when it includes her sister, Lesmosyne. In other words, forgetting is always present and haunts, if you will, all that we recollect and sustain. Forgetting is part of the same family as remembering. Memory's slippage is Lesmosyne's presence. A "union of opposites," then, attends these tendencies in the soul to remember and to forget.

We might ask at this juncture about the organic nature of memories, so much so that they may need their own time to ripen into insights, or into mimetic or mythopoetic resemblances of themselves. Do memories require of themselves to accumulate enough "as-if" energy about them before they are ready to reveal, as Echo reveals to Narcissus, their full import, inflected perhaps differently than the original wording of the experience? Are memories echoic in this regard? Are they feminine, as Mnemosyne reveals? I say this because in the myth, when Narcissus spurns Echo, he rejects remembrance and with it a sense of irony about himself. The loss of memory can be construed as at the same time a loss of the ironic towards oneself, the result being a sustained self-absorption wherein there exists no room for anything else, least of all personal memories or cultural histories.

On the other hand, is forgetting a protective tissue or gauze around certain memories that allow them to incubate over time, finally to reveal themselves when, for example, one says: "My God, I have not thought about X for 20 years." But at this instant it abrupts into view, wishing to be re-membered into one's main plot line. The moments of interruption and abruption are instances of mythic consciousness emerging into the chronos of our existence. Memory and forgetfulness are mythological moments to be attended to. One drinks Lethe's water in the underworld. In moments of self-forgetfulness is the promise of liberation. However, forgiving but not forgetting can keep one clinging to the original offense or affront, continually calling it up to destroy both equilibrium and a desired serenity. Lethe, Kerenyi observes, makes everything disappear that belongs to the dark side of human existence (130). A balanced flow between remembering and forgetting promotes an equilibrium in the soul and serves to keep the waters of conscious being fresh and free of stagnation.

Nicholas Carr's book, *The Shallows: What the Internet is Doing to Our Brains,* was a Pulitzer Prize finalist in 2011. It is a profound study of the power of technology to affect the very basic ways we remember and forget. While the book is too complex to explore here, I want to give some attention to an article he published in *The Atlantic* in November, 2013 entitled "The Great Forgetting."

He begins by recounting several passenger plane crashes caused by "pilot error." Carr identifies these horrific miscalculations as stemming from too much reliance on automation to fly passenger planes such that pilots over time lose the reflexive memories needed to respond to crises when they occur: "Overuse of automation erodes pilots' expertise and dulls their reflexes, leading to what Jan Noyes, an ergonomics expert . . . terms a 'de-skilling of the crew'" (78).

Carr's thesis is that we are naïve when we think that introducing automation simply frees us up to do other things, while remaining completely ignorant of how that automation changes the mind's ability to perform. He refers to such thinking as "the substitution myth" (79). The thinking here leaves out that most important of elements in whatever tasks we perform: Context. He then cites studies of two psychologists who conclude that "'automation does not simply supplant human activity but rather changes it, often in ways unintended and unanticipated by the designers of automation'" (79).

Fully invested in the belief that the machines we use will perform without flaws, Carr claims, we become dull in our level of awareness and in other sources of information like our eyes and ears. I understand what he says here as a form of forgetting; when awareness is narrowed, when a false sense of security gains ascendance, our ability to remember is lowered. In a crisis, panic may be more the norm than remembrance of what one was at one time trained to do in these moments when our softwared machines crash. Finally, Carr believes that "steps to promote the development and maintenance of expertise almost always entails a sacrifice of speed and productivity" (81). These two qualities are such ingrained properties of both our personal and collective myths that surrendering them is extremely difficult and distasteful. Carr believes that only with the slowness of understanding can we become less victims of the very programs we develop to promote both qualities.

Following on his crucial insights into remembering and forgetting, I want to pose the following:

Questions to Consider on Remembering/ Forgetting:

- How might forgetting be understood as an act of consciousness equally as important as remembering?
- What goes into our decision to shred, discard or forget something or someone in our history?
- Can we design rituals of cleaning and cleansing our emotional, historical and psychological house?
- What parts of a fixed version of ourselves are we desirous of forgetting?
- If, in meeting a new person, where might we begin our story to disclose ourselves to that person?
- What details might we be sure to "forget" to tell so as to give our narrative a particular inflection?
- If we were to tell someone who does not know us two qualities, incidents or events in our life that have been extremely memorable, what would they be?
- How does forgetting shape us?
- How might forgetting shame us?
- How might forgetting honor us?
- What looms most large in our life that we believe we are ready to forget?
- What do we seem to insist on remembering that continues to wound us?

Finally, as I continue to teach Dante's magnificent *Commedia,* I am struck by the souls in *Inferno* most. What they seem to carry in their shady substances in all the levels of Hell is of course the absence of God's presence. But on another, more emotional level, their greatest fear is not to be remembered. As Dante speaks to many of them on his pilgrimage through this tortured region, what he is asked most frequently by those shades he knew in this life, is that Dante carry their memory back to the living so they will be recalled and so avoid being relegated to the landscape of oblivion. To be forgotten is to lose a large sense of one's identity; we live so much in the recollections of others and whether we lived a virtuous or a maladaptive life, what we wish to avoid is to be consigned to the waters of Lethe. There may be no greater suffering than the one that oblivion threatens us with. That is worth remembering.

Endnote

[1] Sections of this essay were presented at a conference in County Kerry, Ireland entitled "Memory, Dreams and Reflections" as part of the *Jung In Ireland* series sponsored by the New York Center for Jungian Studies and directed by Aryeh Maidenbaum and Diana Ruben, March 28-April 4, 2014.

Works Cited

Alighieri, Dante. *The Divine Comedy*. Trans. Allen Mandelbaum. Introd. by Eugenio Montale. New York: Alfred A. Knopf, 1995.

Armstrong, Robert Plant. *Wellsprings: On the Myth and Source of Culture*. Berkeley: U California P, 1977.

Borges, Jorge Luis. "Funes the Memorius." *Labyrinths*. Trans. James E. Irby. New York: New Directions, 1964. 148-154.

Campbell, Joseph. *Myths to Live By*. Foreword by Johnson E. Fairchild. New York: Penguin Compass, 1972.

Carr, Nicholas. "The Great Forgetting." *The Atlantic*. November, 2013. 77-81.

Eliade. Mircea. "Mythologies of Memory and Forgetting." *Parabola: Myth, Tradition and the Search for Meaning*. November 1986. 68-75.

Hogan, Linda. *Solar Storms*. New York: Simon and Schuster, 1995.

Homer. *The Odyssey*. Trans. and Ed. Albert Cook. A Norton Critical Edition. New York: Norton, 1974. 3-336.

Huxley, Aldous. *Brave New World and Brave New World Revisited*. Foreword by Christopher Hitchens. New York: HarperPerennial, 2004.

Kerenyi, Karl. "Mnemosyne—Lesmosyne: On the Springs of 'Memory' and 'Forgetting.'" *Spring: An Annual of Archetypal Psychology and Jungian Thought*. The Analytical Psychology Club of New York, Inc., 1977. 120-130.

Lamers, Marianne. "The Importance of Forgetting: Why The Ability to Forget is Essential to Keeping Memories Alive." *Health and*

Healing, July/August 2013. 26-30.

Margalit, Avishai. *The Ethics of Memory*. Cambridge, Mass.: Harvard UP, 2002.

Morrison, Toni. *Beloved*. New York: Knopf, 1992.

Rousseau, Jean-Jacques. *The Confessions*. Trans. J.M. Cohen. New York: Penguin, 1953.

Slattery, Dennis Patrick. *Riting Myth, Mythic Writing: Plotting Your Personal Story*. Skiatook, OK: Fisher King P, 2013.

Spence, Donald P. *Narrative Truth and Historical Truth: Meaning and Interpretation in Psychoanalysis*. New York: Norton, 1982.

Weinrich, Harald. *Lethe: The Art and Critique of Forgetting*. Trans. Steven Rendall. Ithaca: Cornell UP, 2004.

CHAPTER 16

CALLED TO A COHEARANT LIFE

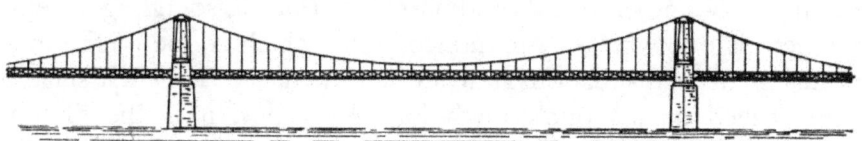

The word "cohere" carries a couple of meanings when one says it aloud rather than reads it silently. It sounds something like "to hear with" or "to listen with." It is a co-operative. A cohearant life is one that enjoys not the absence of conflict, strife or contradiction but an accord of the pieces with some larger organic whole. Joseph Campbell loved the verbs "to be in accord with" or "to correspond with." They captured for him some agreement, even a contract, between parts that promoted a living and vibrant wholeness. In *Myths to Live By* he suggests that "it has always been on myths that the moral orders of societies have been founded." From this insight Campbell affirms "the imagery of myths to be life-enhancing" (11).

Contrary to what contemporary culture insists we believe, namely, that economics in the form of capital and monetary interests are or should be the platinum bar in the bureau of standards for both study and work, Campbell countered that each of us "organizes his life according primarily to mythic and only secondarily to economic laws and aims" (21). But myth and its necessity is being muffled and gagged by the glut of money; the irony here of course is that economics itself is a myth. It derives from the Greek word, *oikos*, the home, the land, the entirety of one's domicile, from which we derive our word economics, which meant originally the proper ordering and running of the household. It is thus in culture the complement to the polis, what we now call the city. When *oikos* and household are in harmony, or in accord with one another, we experience the balanced worlds of home and city in sweet agreement—*sophrosyne.* In short, they agreeably cohere. Perhaps this coherence arises because they hear what the other needs and desires to fulfill its nature to accommodate it.

Campbell's own version of *Moby-Dick*, his white whale, is *The Hero With a Thousand Faces* published in 1949. With its public appearance, he began a rise to stardom; he was officially on the mythic map, although as you know, many dismissed him as popular and therefore unsuitable as a scholar. Envy indeed takes many forms but has only one end. In his admittedly formulaic-sounding schema, the hero is one who is "summoned" (56), which is one of the most primal archetypal situations individuals can engage. This first stage of being called begins one's mythological journey; it is the **Call to Adventure,** which "summons the hero and transfers his spiritual center of gravity within the pale of his society to a zone unknown" (58). C.G. Jung would call this very moment the start of one's process of individuation, a journey towards wholeness. Such a condition is not for the faint of heart, for to enter the zone that promises little security or predictability is to risk everything in its purchase. One better be prepared to leave home with nothing, or to return much lighter than one left.

Now let's pause for a moment to draw a straight line from Campbell's great study of the Hero directly to one of C.G. Jung's most important and life-changing volumes of his *Collected Works*, *Symbols of Transformation*, which he tells us in the "Foreword to the Fourth Swiss Edition" was written "in 1911, in my thirty-sixth year" (xxvi). He informs us of this fact 37 years later as he recollects the volume's value for him. We might remember here that he writes the bulk—some 2/3 of *The Red Book* between October 1912 and March 1913, so he is on the cusp of working that magnificent book into life soon after finishing *Symbols.*

I want to draw this straight line between two expansive and insightful volumes on myth because of what Jung himself informs us of in his own life at this time in his 75th year. Here is where I increase my own interest in the Foreword of 1950:

> Hardly had I finished the manuscript when it struck me what it means to live with a myth, and what it means to live without one. Myth, says a Church Father, is "what is believed always, everywhere, by everybody"; hence the man who thinks he can live without myth, or outside it, is an exception. He is like one uprooted, having no true link either with the past, or with the ancestral life which continues within him. (xxiv)

History, the form of the past we give shape to, disappears within a mythless life. Jung does not yet want to let this sense of mythlessness go; he continues: "So I suspected that myth had a meaning which I was sure to miss if I lived outside it in the haze of my own speculations" (xxiv). He then poses to himself the fundamental question whose energy motivates my current presentation: "I was driven to ask myself in all seriousness: 'What is the myth you are living?' I found no answer to this question, and had to admit that I was not living with a myth, or even in a myth, but rather in an uncertain cloud of theoretical possibilities which I was beginning to regard with increasing distrust" (xxiv-xxv). I think we can see the call behind Jung's words as well as the consternation and confusion about living a life outside of a mythic sensibility. He is, I suspect, being summoned at just this juncture of questioning with ever-growing dissatisfaction and even distrust of what he had until this moment, believed in.

Now to question is to begin the quest. It is to interrogate, to seek or hunt down a response. Being called is to be called *forth* to begin the journey, which is Jung's position here at age 75. He continues his self-interrogation: "I did not know that I was living a myth, and even if I had known it, I would not have known what sort of myth was ordering my life without my knowledge. So, in the most natural way, I took it upon myself to get to know 'my' myth and I regarded it as the task of tasks" (xxv).

More can be cited here, but the above is sufficient to launch us into the second part of this address. Notice that he recognizes one of the main tenets of a myth: it is an ordering principle, a way of giving the parts of our often disparate existence a form; myths are formative standards that help us to live a coherent life, not to eliminate from it strife or challenge or suffering. It is rather to organize them and other elements into discernible patterns of thought and response.

Let's return to Joseph Campbell's thinking about myth from a work mentioned above, *Myths to Live By*, one of his more vernacular creations for a larger interested audience. There he relates that "a myth is a foundational set of beliefs that help an individual in his/her life, or an entire nation, found what moral order, what set of values they choose to adhere to, to defend" (44). But we might also note that a life can become incoherent and maladaptive as well as coherent by a myth; the former when it creates such dissension, such friction in its fiction in our lives that it best be dropped. A myth that has outlived its purpose in guiding one to a sense of wholeness and accord with self and world is one that has likely calcified into a suffocating set of dogmatic assertions. A myth should enhance life, not desecrate it; the patterns of thought that typify myths we each might best examine periodically and question to see what is still operative for the individual, or the common good, and what has frozen and become sclerotic and arthritic. Those of you who suffer from arthritis know that one of its key limitations is that it restricts motion, end-stops movement; in its presence we lose flexibility. So too with an arthritic mythos; glucosamine is insufficient to return elasticity.

I remember some years ago having the pleasure of teaching a four day course on myth, both personal and collective, with Jungian analyst Marion Woodman at Eranos in Switzerland during a summer program sponsored by Pacifica Graduate Institute. I taught the writing piece and Marion led us in body movement to cultivate a keener mythic consciousness. One of her insights has stayed with me over others I heard that week: Wisdom is the capacity to know which parts of our personal myth are healthy and operative for us and what parts need to be jettisoned, let go of, dismissed as no longer of value. That's a pretty accurate paraphrase. She and I were, each in our own way, attempting to open that portal of awareness that Jung realized in his 75th year.

Perhaps the Persian poet Jelaluddin Rumi (1207-1273) captures it best; it is no accident that he remains today the best-selling poet in the United States. Here is a section of one of his most famous poems:

Unfold Your Own Myth

.... Who, like Jacob blind with grief and age,
smells the shirt of his lost son
and can see again?
Who lets a bucket down and brings up
 a flowing prophet? Or like Moses goes for fire
And finds what burns inside the sunrise?
....
But don't be satisfied with stories, how things
Have gone with others. Unfold
 your own myth, without complicated explanation,
So everyone will understand the passage,
We have opened you. . . . *(The Essential Rumi* 40-41)

Rumi both celebrates us in the unfolding of our own myth and cautions us against living another's myth in its stead. Myths do indeed call us—they call us to a work and to a life. One of the greatest sadnesses that can befall us as mythic mammals is to approach the end of our life and realize that we have lived out another's myth, have followed the path of a parent, sibling, a friend or a stranger and never trodden where there is no path, which is the genesis in space of one's own authentic path. Now that individual's own children may inherit a double burden: first to live out the myth that the parent refused, so they put their own mythic journey on hold. Second, they then move with whatever time remains to hear and respond to their own calling. It is a terrible burden to be placed in such a double bind to two myths, each insisting on one's attention.

While I did not plan what follows, I want to be true to it. Before I had reread Rumi's poem for consideration in this talk,[1] when I turned my attention to this presentation while sitting quietly in my study at 4 a.m. and meditating on it, the image from *Exodus* of the miraculous burning bush that does not consume itself emerged like a rainbow trout from the depths of a stream. You remember in the above poem that Rumi addresses Moses "who goes for fire/and finds what burns inside the sunrise?" No accident here; so what follows is my return to Exodus to witness Moses begin to unfold his own myth.

We each have sensed at various moments in our lives when we were in the presence of something far bigger and grander than ourselves. Most often it visits in times of solitude or solidarity with others, or in sickness either of body or soul—at times of affliction. I believe these are poetic instances of being called, a call to the myth that insists we live it. When I say "poetic instances," I refer to the origin of the word, *poiesis,* which is a making or a shaping, a sculpting of sorts, of something unformed into a coherent form that can be made public and shared. We may have had parents or others say to us in a given circumstance: "Make something of yourself or of your life." That is a statement of *poiesis*—it is a call to create, which some of you may recognize is the title of Jungian analyst Linda Leonard's excellent book on creativity.

So *poiesis* is a crafting of ourselves into a form. I think that form embodies a felt sense of co-hearance: we listen closely in silence and hear something. We are moving through the world and we come to a burning bush that does not consume itself; out from its benevolent flames emerges a voice. I want to entertain the idea that it is a voice of co-hearance. Recall for a moment with me the second book of the Hebrew Bible, *Exodus,* which we are told is the record of Israel's birth as a nation (60); but as we read it closely, we see that such a birth requires an antecedent; that antecedent is the birth of Moses, and it arrives in the form of a voice first in the appearance of an angel of the Lord, who appears to him in a flame of fire in the midst of a bush (Ex. 3:2). Now one may call it a miraculous flame because it does not consume what it has engulfed. I can go with that, but want to add that it is a mythic flame, perhaps even the presence of the flame of myth itself. It is the flame of awareness, of presentness and it appears along the path that Moses is walking. The flame is no longer following the dictates of nature's law but of another world's format. It is the flame that arouses curiosity, that stops one in one's tracks to ponder mystery itself; that is why I think it is the flame of myth. Stay with a myth long enough, and its finger will point you towards mystery, the ineffable, even, for Campbell, the mystical and the transcendent. That language captures his version as well of the *unus mundus.*

Moses attempts to look at the bush burning; God's voice calls to him from the midst of it: "Moses, Moses," and he answered, "here I am" (3:3). We can puzzle over why God calls his name twice—are there at this instance two Moses, the one who is about to perish and the other who is about to begin a life more fully unfolding his own myth? Nonetheless, God tells him He has come to deliver His people out of Egypt, to a land flowing with those archetypal wonders of the palette: milk and honey.

Then he calls on Moses to be the instrument of this Divine plan. Moses' response is as rich as the milk and honey: "Who am I that I should go to Pharaoh, that I should bring the children of Israel, out of Egypt?" "Who am I?" is crucial, for he does not know; we might recall Jung's own puzzling over who he is and what his myth implicates. For being called is a moment of instrumental import, when one is willing to be an instrument of something one is called to do and to be. Such a yielding, myths reveal, often leads to a fuller sense of self's identity. Campbell reminds us that when the hero heeds the call, s/he makes an act of the will to give oneself over to something beyond the self in that vocation. It is a vocative moment; being willing to be instrumental, but not incidental, is the crucial instance of yielding that originates the formation of a coherent life. In Exodus resides the shards of Genesis.

Coherence is the by-product of a destiny; destiny is the occasion of a willing response to something outside oneself and at the same time is the noblest impulse within. As out there, so in here, to paraphrase Heraclitus. Thus initially, Moses asks "Who am I?" which brings into question his entire complex identity, to which God tells him what to do, not how to be: "Gather the elders of Israel together; tell them you will bring them out of the affliction of Egypt to a land of Canaanites and others" (3:4). To be called, the story intimates, may be to heal a wound, an affliction, or an injustice; one's orbit expands out of oneself to embrace others; in that act alone is a profound liberation from self-absorption as well as from personal needs and desires.

God continues by informing Moses they will heed his voice; but Moses' doubts detain his acceptance of the calling: "But suppose they will not believe me or listen to my voice; suppose they say 'the Lord has not appeared to you'?" (4:1). In response, the Lord then offers Moses a sign: He tells him to drop the rod he carries onto the ground. When he obeys, the rod immediately morphs into a serpent. Moses picks it up by the tail, at which it suddenly turns back into a rod. Startled by this incident, but still at a distance from conversion, he then seeks another excuse to avoid the call: "But I am not eloquent neither before or since you have spoken to your servant. I am slow of speech and slow of tongue" (4:10).

Something new opens here in this vocation; precisely where Moses believes he is deficient is the exact soft spot in himself he must enter to create a coherent life by the action of freeing his people. Any journey into the world is simultaneously a pilgrimage into one's own interior, Campbell observes repeatedly as he explores the stories of world mythologies.

I would italicize here that vocation is a form of vacation: one is called to vacate one's own plans or one's self-absorption or fear-based hesitation, and to enter into the spirit of another, to expand more plausibly into his/her full nature, which occurs when one has enough heart (courage) to relinquish it. Now we are deeply enmeshed in the terrain of myth. Where our soft spot is, where we feel most deficient, vulnerable and perhaps unworthy marks the territory we must step into. I bet you each have your stories of this paradoxical moment in your own formation. Destiny does not often play to one's strengths but to one's vulnerabilities; part of the reason that a true calling is so transformative is its insistence in pushing us to confront the less vital, more imperfect aspects of our being. In that sense our defects are inroads into our destiny. Moses' fear overcomes him at this moment: "Lord, please send someone by the hand of whoever else you may send" (4:13). The Lord grows impatient with Moses' insistent deflection of his destiny and continues to persist. He calls up Moses' brother Aaron. "I know he can speak well. He comes to meet you. Now you shall speak to him and put the words in his mouth. And I will be with your mouth and with his mouth, and I will teach you what you shall do" (4:15).

From mouth to mouth is a mythic move. I realize I am jumping from the Hebraic to the Greek world in what follows. In Greek, *muthos* means mouth and is the origin of the word mythos. So when we open our mouth to speak, we are exhaling our muthos. If we allow such a leap to the Greek etymology of the word myth, then what we speak to another is co-heard; in the process one's own muthos coheres in the hearing. No matter what we say or how we say it, our lexical landscape is brought into enactment. We note that Moses' brother Aaron is to be Moses' mouthpiece, even his myth-piece, his spokesman; so the following equation emerges:

God – Moses
becomes
Moses – Aaron

As Moses is God's instrument, so Aaron is Moses' instrument; the divine-human coherence is now replicated or mimed in the human-human conjoining. As the Lord observes, "So he shall be your spokesman to the people. And he himself shall be as a mouth for you, and you shall be to him as God" (4:16).

What are we to discern here? To be called is not an act in isolation even while it may take place in solitude. It is more one of communion, of *communitas* in the word of anthropologist Victor Turner (*The Ritual Process* 111). We are beckoned or summoned into elevating ourselves beyond our self-imposed limits. I believe that to be called is not only vocational but fundamentally an act of faith, to which each of us is required to make a leap. "And Aaron spoke all the words that which the Lord had spoken to Moses" (4:30). Aaron echoes the words of God that Moses heard earlier and related to his brother. Perhaps Aaron's calling occurs at the same time; one's being called may be a private event but its consequences are always public. Our calling is not only to a content of doing but to a context of being and then, further out, of being-in-relation.

The exchange above reveals that we are con-textual beings; the texture of our lives in and out of callings will very often involve others: communal, collegial and connatural. As with the case of God, Moses and his brother, this trinity forms what C.G. Jung calls an archetypal situation: "Interpretations are only for those who don't understand; it is only the things we don't understand that have any meaning: (*Collected Works* 9,1 ¶65). It is in addition one of transformation, for to be called is often an invitation to enter the wilderness, the desert, the forest or the unknown landscape—the terrain of fairy tales, myths, legends and classic works of literature and film.

The call we receive is not the road of comforts, clear street signs and well-lit bolstering arrows pointing us to the right route or the most secure direction. Rather, it is to enter the woods where no clear path exists; otherwise we have responded to another's call if the path is already visible. The caution at this moment is not to spend time on what you can sense is a decoy from your true path. If you wish to study depth psychology more deeply, do it. A candidate for the myth program this fall wrote in his personal statement: "I have started to apply for the myth program three times previously. Now I know it is time to slay the dragon." His soul has moved from hearing to heeding; I think this motion also involves some level of healing, for one is now willing to negotiate the lived terms of one's soul. Soul life is both a risky as well as a frisky business.

In addition, and to shift a bit in time and space, I am intrigued by the opening of another narrative which uses biblical figures and themes throughout: the narrative of the great white whale, *Moby-Dick*, which begins with the pithy address, **Call** me Ishmael (3).

When we read these three words aloud, as a calling, we are Ishmael—as echo. As Aaron echoes Moses, and Moses echoes God, so too do we give up or moderate our believed in and beloved path in order to become another. Read another way, Call **me** Ishmael, we seek to be called by the other, not just called the other. Call just me please and no other. We seek to be called by the other, the castaway, the illegitimate, the marginal—who in the case of Ishmael will become a leader of nations. In Hebrew Ishmael means "God shall hear." And the third: Call me **Ishmael**. My name may be Frank or Oswald, Marie or Sandy, but for this narrative call me this name because it fits the plot of the occasion.

The last call, from a time closer to our own is that of the German poet Rainer Maria Rilke, who began responding to a series of letters written by a young army officer, a 19 year old aspiring poet, Franz Xaver Kappas. These exchanges have been gathered in a small collection of 10 missives called *Letters to a Young Poet*. They are less about the craft of writing poems and more on the call to create poetry. It makes us ponder how what we are called to is itself a project, as I think these letters reveal.

The first letter to Rilke is 17 February of 1903. To the question Franz poses to the poet about even writing poetry, Rilke responds: "Go into yourself. Find out the reason that commands you to write. See whether it has spread its roots into the very depths of your heart; confess to yourself whether you would have to die if you were forbidden to write; this most of all: ask yourself in the most silent hour of your night: *must* I write?" (3).

The litmus test for a life's work congeals in this response; one's life depends on engaging what beckons. It is a summons to meaning and purpose. One has the choice to refuse the call, as Joseph Campbell relates it. Then one risks engaging an existence within an unlived life, free of the organizing principle of one's personal myth. I suspect that such a life is what Jung referred to earlier as being unmoored in life, of having no roots, no grounding, of being, essentially, not of this earth.

Later in the letter Rilke is harsh: ("if, as I have said, one feels one could live without writing, then one shouldn't write at all") (10). We may not need to be so tendentious, but the poet's words strike at the non-negotiable quality of a calling. I have listened to many people over the years, who, when the conversation drifted to different topics and life trajectories, would say: "someday I hope to…" or "I always wanted to. . . but it seemed so impractical so. . . . " Jung himself felt the fear for a good part of his life of inhabiting an unlived life, which is to say a life with little or no meaning, one that added up to nothing. His incredible striving can be understood as his response to such a fear.

Later, towards the end of the series of letters, Rilke turns to the absolute gift and importance of solitude as one searches for the feeling of authenticity that companions one's calling: "What is necessary, after all, is only this: solitude, vast inner solitude. To walk inside yourself and meet no one for hours—that is what you must be able to attain" (54). I like this observation because it provides an antibody or antidote to the world toxin that dictates the career path, the mythic journey of a life; one acquiesces to the cultural demands to the exclusion of the soul's longing for and need to follow a different, more authentic path. Solitude provides a bulwark, a quiet temenos in which one may meditate, pray and reflect on what life, not the surrounding mass-produced demands and values, is asking of one. These spaces of solitude can be life-transforming as prologues to the next step: engaging the myth that unfolds from within.

Campbell liked to repeatedly use the image of one climbing the ladder of success only to discover that the ladder itself was not in error; it just happened to be leaning up against the wrong wall. Now that shock of recognition can be devastating to the soul of the individual. In that period of teaching with Marion Woodman at Eranos, she related the story to the group of a previous workshop working with older women and their individual paths. In one exercise, she asked each to assume a bodily position that most captured each of their present situations in life. As the participants began to move around the room, thinking of their body gestures and postures, one woman in her mid-70s lay on the floor and curled herself into a fetal position and began to weep uncontrollably. Later, as the women were asked if they wanted to tell their story that was captured in their gestural bodies, this same woman, through a veil of tears, related that only recently had she come to realize that she had lived someone else's life, not her own. Her fetal position mirrored her deep yearning to be reborn so she could more faithfully live her own life rightly this second time. She knew she had ransomed her own calling to the wishes of others.

Ease, safety, security, certainty—these are the bromides of our world today. But they can be deadening to a call where one responds: "Call me back; I'm busy."

When Rilke responds to Franz about his writing, he observes:

> Most people have, (with the help of conventions) turned their solutions toward what is easy and toward the less conflictual side of the easy; but it is clear that we must trust in what is difficult; everything alive trusts in it, everything in Nature grows and defends itself any way it can, is spontaneously itself, tries to be itself to itself at all costs and against all opposition…we must trust in what is difficult. (67-68)

Called to a cohearant life is both a gift and a grit. Doing anything less will leave one in the desert at the end of a life—having hoped for x and desired a bunch of y's, yet never assenting authentically to the call. Here we cannot call collect; we must heed the call and pay for it with a lifetime of honoring its persistent, divine and engaging presence. Only then can we say at the end: I lived the life I was put on this earth to engage.

Endnote

[1] This essay was presented as the Annual Saybrook University Jungian Studies Honorary Lecture, Houston Jung Education Center, Houston Texas, November 7, 2014.

Works Cited

Campbell, Joseph. *Myths to Live By.* Foreword by Johnson E. Fairchild. New York: Penguin Compass, 1993.

---. *The Hero With a Thousand Faces.* Third Edition. Bollingen Series XVII. Novato, California: New World Library, 2008.

Holy Bible: Containing the Old and New Testaments. New King James Version. New York: Nelson Bibles, 1982.

Jung, C.G. *Symbols of Transformation: An Analysis of the Prelude to a Case of Schizophrenia.* Second Ed. Trans. R.F.C. Hull. *The Collected Works of C.G. Jung,* vol. 5. Princeton: Princeton UP, 1956.

---. *Archetypes and the Collective Unconscious.* Second Ed. Trans. R.F.C. Hull. *The Collected Works of C.G. Jung,* vol. 9,$_1$. Princeton: Princeton UP, 1968.

Melville, Herman. *Moby-Dick; or, The Whale.* Introduction by Clifton Fadiman. Illustrations by Boardman Robinson. Norwalk, Connecticut: The Easton Press, 1977.

Rilke, Rainer Maria. *Letters to a Young Poet.* Trans. Stephen Mitchell. New York: The Modern Library, 1984.

Rumi, Jellaladin. *The Essential Rumi.* Trans. Coleman Barks, with John Moyne, et. al. Edison, NJ: Castle Books, 1997.

Turner, Victor. *The Ritual Process: Structure and Anti-Structure.* Foreword by Roger D. Abrahams. New Brunswick: AldineTransaction, 2008.

CHAPTER 17

THE MYTH OF MEMORIAL DAY

Another Memorial Day has become an additional memory in our cultural heritage. What this day of remembrance means for us as a nation is so crucial to our national identity that we have memorialized it as part of our country's essential calendar. But one could ask: why is it so important and in some way, so necessary? I propose that what is never brought up for acknowledgement in this or any national holiday's importance is its mythic power and persistence, even its durability because of the values it carries for so many Americans. Coupled with its persistence is the question of why the many rituals we employ each year as markers for our collective memories must be maintained and honored.

Now most people would say today, given the media's use of the term, that a myth is nothing more than a lie, a falsehood, an untruth. We see the term in ads and in newspaper and magazine articles, most all of which announce that myths are the opposite of facts and truth. Few would know that such a definition is itself the product of a myth, the Myth of Enlightenment thought in 18th century Western Europe and shipped to the United States. Enlightenment thought pervaded and guided the imaginations of our Founding Fathers and is securely ensconced in the original documents that crafted in words our nascent identity as a people who sought freedom from British tyranny. We are the children of this period in history that promoted the following beliefs: 1. Reason is the only sure path to the truth. Science here is our guiding mantra to help us reach this pristine state; 2. The imagination is an unsafe pathway to the truth and so should not be taken seriously, nor should its products, which more often than not foster falsehoods; 3. Knowledge itself can be organized, categorized and put into slots to be more easily retrieved. The Enlightenment gave us both the dictionary and the encyclopedia as organizers of knowledge. These books were in important ways the precursor to our current technology and its step-child, the world wide web.

However, for eons before this historical period, myths, folklore, legends, narratives, fables and fairy tales were understood to be both viable and often preferred forms of knowing. But with the rise of reason, rationality, analysis and computation in the Enlightenment period, the Western Imagination lost its fidelity to or belief in myth; however, it did not foreclose on mythic moments in its history, nor did it lose the accompanying rituals that embody and give shape and action to those mythic situations that carry us back historically to the founding of something or to the making sacred of an event or national epoch. Memorial Day is one such ritual pause to remember something we hold as representing great value for both our identity and continuity. Perhaps the most popular mythologist of the current epoch is Joseph Campbell (1904-87), whose *Power of Myth* series on PBS has been watched by millions since its first airing in 1988. In one of his most forceful books, *Myths to Live By*, he notes that "it has always been on myths that the moral orders of societies have been founded" (11). In fact, as he relates some pages later, "to look at man from a psychological rather than physical attributes reveals that man organizes his life according primarily to mythic, and only secondarily, to economic aims and laws" (22). We know this bold statement would receive resolute push-back by many today who are so ensconced in the myth of The Market that they can see nothing else of real value to pursue or cultivate. That is how powerful a myth can be; it can blind one to all other options as it promotes a belief that only this or that value is of any import.

I think, following on some of Campbell's insights, that a myth serves three functions for not only an individual, but for a tribe, a community and even an entire nation: 1. A myth *sustains* us. It does so by holding and furthering through organic growth, values and beliefs that define our identity and assure their central place in a national consciousness. Countries enter wars with others in order to protect and even disseminate their own most vitalizing myths. 2. A myth *restrains* us. When we live individually or nationally within an organic and living myth, we allow ourselves to do and say certain things while muting or refraining from other forms of behavior and expression. Some we actually pass laws prohibiting. The laws we create and uphold and enforce are all predicated on certain mythic constants. Look to a country's or an individual's laws and mores and one sees the general and specific ligaments of their mythos. Without boundaries, an individual or a nation can be formidably dangerous to self and others. 3. A myth *explains* us. What we hold most alive in our lives gives us meaning, coherence and a desire to cultivate our talents and our deepest interests. Without a myth, one has no real identity; one can lose this essential element that makes one uniquely human by simply following the whims, ideologies and prejudices of others. To follow such worn paths is never to step on to one's own; identity becomes a shadow of who one is, and not a substance. Periodically during the year, therefore, we pause and re-collect our mythic roots, even our mythic routes, for it is an on-going journey with many discernable paths that we consciously and at time unconsciously pursue.

Here is a simple writing exercise that would allow you to tap something of your personal myth: When you wake in the morning, ask yourself this question: "What do I assume about myself and today that is going to get me out of bed and moving?" Write out your response. Then go to the other side: "What do I assume about myself and today that I wish I did not assume for it makes me want to stay in bed?" Answering both of these positive and negative assumptions will identify something fundamental about your personal myth. Assumptions are mythic beliefs that have slipped under the floorboard of consciousness, but for all that, they exert powerful holds on our worldview and on what we engage that hold us to our intentions, our likes and our purpose.

Works Cited

Campbell, Joseph. *Myths to Live By*. Foreword by Johnson E. Fairchild. New York: Penguin Compass, 1993.

CHAPTER 18

GROWTH: WHEN A MYTH NO LONGER SERVES

I have read with great appreciation the last few weeks the "Letters to the Editor" decrying the number of new building permits issued by the city of New Braunfels for both private dwellings and office buildings. Today's "Opinion" essay: "SOS: Save Our Springs," (19 August 2014) is another iteration of the same need for radical conservation in both water usage as well as on the size of the population in this region that is sustainable. Pretending abundance when in drought conditions is both irresponsible and unethical. In fact, it is downright dangerous.

While these letters of caution and alarm, given the immediate and longer range necessity of conserving water, have been accurate, they have failed to touch the deeper question: what myth is it that compels the engines of growth? Until the underlying myth that shapes the thinking of what a people value is addressed, the problem stays above ground and tends to draw to itself ways of fixing something. Fixing as solution is also a mythic structure, but it will have to wait for another essay to delineate its limited terms.

The language of growth, development, expansion, bigger, more, enlargement, Manifest-Destiny are all terms highlighting the same value. If then myths, both personal and collective, are mediums of value, then they can also direct us to what is not valued and best dropped into the wastebasket of forgetting. As responsible citizens, we have to be very vigilant in order to designate and acknowledge who it is that makes such critical determinations. For what we are asked or persuaded to dis-remember is as powerful a force as what we are told or forced to remember. Development, increase, expansion, enlargement have been core elements of America's values since their inception. History reveals that much has been done constructively and destructively to satisfy the appetites of these values. What we do as individuals and as a culture to enact, so to more firmly remember, the myths we hold closest to our identity become evident in the form of rituals. Rituals embody, incarnate and bequeath integrity to what we believe to be true and necessary for our own identity, respect and growth.

But myths, like anything else that is organic, including us, wear out, break down and eventually expose an expired shelf-life date. If the myths we hold sacred prove no longer operative, constructive, helpful or that at times, given changing circumstances, require moderation, revisiting or revisioning, they will undergo change only if they are truly vibrant and organic; but if they have instead calcified into some brittle form of dogmatic assertion or absolute truth to the exclusion of any other options or possibilities that are more in tune with the current realities surrounding us, then the myth is closer to the condition of a cadaver than a living value. Looking, then, below the surface of changes we wish to make as a community, such as growth, by inviting others into the state or region because of a lower tax base, we see the myth driving such expansion is not only unreasonable but an immoral act. Denying the mythic reality resting below the literal reality of this or that policy or public action, like signing off on an increasing number of developers' permits, is both naïve and harmful to the body politic's survival.

One more observation. Consider a time historically when hunter-gatherer people had to pay sharp attention to the climate, to weather patterns and to the designs of migrating herds, their major food source; failure to do so meant the difference between starvation or survival. Staying in touch with the Environment, noting its shifting patterns, may require a shift in the myths that we give value through. Such is the case with Development.

The myth of Development need not be erased; but it does require re-tooling and modification. By itself it is NOT a virtue; it needs tending and cultivating, pruning back and moderating its growth. Failure to do so is the result of two devastating weapons that are hard to expunge: Ignorance and Arrogance. Arrogance says "I need not pay attention to the world around me because I am in charge and have my own interests to promote"; Ignorance says "I do not need to know what will be the long term effects of new territory I enter because things have worked just fine in the past." Both Ignorance and Arrogance are witness to a frozen imagination that disregards the primal nature of our species as myth-makers and changers.

A healthy society is one that continually reevaluates its mythic roots and shoots that give it life; history reveals with uncanny repetition that disaster eventuates often when an old myth stubbornly attempts to serve a changed world that no longer responds to it. Denial, too, is a mistaken mythic response to impending disaster because of scarcity.

CHAPTER 19

POETRY AS FRAME AND AS FORM

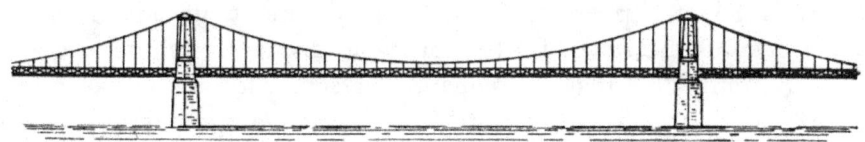

Creating this volume of poetry with two other poets and longtime friends[1] is a joy and an opportunity. As we each agreed to write an Introduction to our selection of poems, we have an opportunity to muse on the act of *poiesis,* of making and shaping poems into existence through an imaginal act. I hope to write a few ideas here that have not had a chance to air until now; they are deeply subjective, incomplete, open-ended and not particularly supported in any scholarly way. Perhaps the poems that follow it will give more credence to these observations. If not, then I have more work yet to do. Consider them then more as musings than as proofs or explanations or descriptions of poetry or of poems themselves.

The very popular cognitive linguist George Lakoff's politically-inflected book, *Don't Think of an Elephant!* offers an understanding of the elections of 2000 and 2004. His controlling metaphor is that of the frame. Rereading it recently, I thought of how poetry itself is a form of linguistic framing, not for political but for psycho-aesthetic purposes. His insights have led me to think of the way in which poetry frames the world. It forces me to reassess the notion that windows to the world have power. Rather, the power resides in the frame the window glass clings to for support and stability. A sheet of glass with no frame is relatively useless, but a frame without a sheet of glass loses little potency. Frames remain faithful to the world view they both structure and contain through the boundary they establish. Frames both bound and beatify one piece of the world's arena; they attend to its shaping. If a frame is an opening or a corridor into a world view, then frames structure consciousness itself to see in a certain way and from a particular point of view. There is enormous power in such a structure.

A frame is also a fidelity and a focal point. It is faithful to a way of understanding one thing and everything at once. A poem, I am beginning to appreciate with a bit more clarity, is a frame; it can be one with or without glass. Poetics may then be an aesthetic act of framing the world into a world view. Its optional optics are infinite. Every word in a poem, its structural placement, its advantageous angle, secures the frame further, or it can dismantle it, one side at a time. A frame also makes poignantly present with additional power what lacks this quality when outside it. As such, a frame is an angle of perceiving; what it captures and embraces as well is an attitude towards what its subject matter is. A frame can make the familiar appear fantastic, phenomenal and wondrous.

The work area or space in which frames are constructed is the imagination itself. The poet W.B. Yeats called this space "the rag and bone shop of the heart" (qtd. in *Rag* xvii). The heart, not the head, is the organ that organizes a frame's construction. Yes, the intellect is involved, as is memory, fantasy, anticipations, surmises and of course, craft; these, however, are the implements, the tools that inspire construction. But the heart of a poem resides in the language that frames its design and content. With the heart at its center, it is guaranteed an embodiment that perhaps did not exist before.

The possibilities for the frame are so numerous. Here are a few possibilities. The frame can consist of: an attitude, a belief, a feeling, an insight, a prejudice, an ignorance, a moral certitude, an arresting image. As such, poems as frames can support our ability to focus. Without a frame, for instance, we would move through each day as in a fog; everything would remain opaque, a blur, absent a clear vision. All would run together in a lava flow of unclarity. Frames form our vision, for good or ill. Our habitual patterns in life that no longer benefit us consist of frames that remain stuck in place, rebuffing our attempts to give up their space and influence. Poetry, if taken to heart, offers us new frames by revealing what frames are folly while discerning those whose shelf-life is long expired.

Moreover, a poem can pose the most crucial of questions to us as readers and as creators of it. For instance: when does a frame need dismantling, is no longer of assistance in our own development and actually arrests our awareness rather than expands or deepens it? Now we are into the territory of mytho-poiesis because we have introduced into the frame the presence of myth. Myths are both informing principles as well as energy fields that poetry offers us through metaphor, symbol and analogy. Poems can and do become vessels of energy that guide us to what is most vital in our lives; they do so by the power invested in analogy, in likeness, in similarity. Each one of these terms puts us in touch with a different form of framing. As a point or locus from which to view the world's matter, a frame is a form of understanding. Through such an act of imagination, change is possible and probable.

In both writing poetry and in reading the masters of this art form, some essential elements that comprise us are forged and framed and even re-framed. Writing and reading I understand here to be critical rituals of imagination wherein our emotional, psychological, spiritual and embodied life is given a new form, another way of grasping coherence and shaping memories from our past events. Writing and reading are two of the most essential and enjoyable forms of framing we have as human beings to construct and then view the world by means of them. I know some writers who always write with a blank wall in front of them; I on the other hand write with a window in front of me, its frame a companion to my own thoughts and words.

Pushing off from the metaphor of the frame, I wish to say a few things about form; there is first of all an intimate and friendly relationship between frame and form. Poetry seems to offer the forms of things through their phenomenal appearances in "as-if" framing constructions. A poem's fictional nature is not a limitation to our experience that it contains in some, often new forms. In fact, it is precisely their fictional nature that transports us closer to their truth than any concept could hope to realize. It can do this through a human capacity that the ancient Greeks, most particularly, Aristotle, discovered about poetry: its capacity for mimesis, or imitation on a profound level. Mimesis is a unitary act of imagination as well as a mirroring, so we are able to sense something "by means of." In other words, the physical reality of the poem guides us to the metaphysical dimension of the things of the world in their elemental transcendence. The frame of the poem leads us to the form of ontology that is present but requires a shift in vision to discern it. Seems like a lot. So another way of understanding this phenomenon may be helpful.

Lakoff, cited earlier, is also a neuro-linguist who studies the relation between neural activity and language. To my mind, he illustrates the phenomenon of mimesis biologically: "Each of us, in the premotor cortex of our brains, has what are called mirror neurons. Such neurons fire either when we perform an action or when we see the same action performed by someone else. There are connections from that part of the brain to the emotional centers. Such neural circuits are believed to be the basis of empathy" (54). An astonishing discovery.

Following his insight, if we experience an event performed, which of course happens in reading poetry, what occurs is a response to what we witness "as-if" we had performed it ourselves. Learning, on this level is mimetic, because we imitate the action "as-if" it were personally enacted. We mirror it or imitate it "as-if" it were true. I would say that all art rests on this insight of mimesis that Aristotle gave voice to in his *Poetics* as an act of imagination and which Lakoff millennia later voices as a specific physiological activity of neural functioning. I do not think this is the same as "vicarious" experience, a term I have never liked because it implies a "substitute" reality; rather, what is voiced here is that the imagination does not care whether I performed an act directly, had an insight, or witnessed it through the expression of another. All are equally significant and valued. Mirror neurons carry a mimetic thrust to all of our experiences. Neurologically, the "fictional" nature of an event is not the least impediment to its value and power; what is most decisive is that the event has what humanistic anthropologist Robert Armstrong call affecting presence, a vitality, a power, and a meaning that digs deeply into us (*Wellspring* 13). His point, so essential here, is that a work of art is not a re-presentation but indeed a presentation of being. Given the right frame, crafted with an aesthetic mandate, that deeper sense of our ontic condition will be made available.

In composing a poem or in reading poetry, both carry the capacity to resonate some equivalence, some correspondence, in me, the creator or reader, through its form and its frame. We might recall at this instant the mythologist Joseph Campbell's keen insight: "Metaphor is the native tongue of myth" (*Thou Art That* 48). Metaphor is the form and myth is its frame. If we can enter the poem's energetic field through the aperture of the contemplative act, we may move closer to the archetypal realm out of which the images emanate so to illuminate our darkened consciousness.

As I enter and translate the poem's action, what I eventually make of the poem grows out of my "as-if" mode of consciousness, which is to say the myth I am in, the frame I see through, or by means of. So the myth that guides my mind, imagination and memory as well as "thoughts-about" what I am creating/reading is both personal and collective. I am going for broke here in suggesting that a poem has an internal energy system which, I sense, corresponds to energy systems of the reader's personal myth. Reading is a rite of passage into these fields or systems. They are akin to power centers that exist throughout the person and the poem. What transpires in these centers is the distillation of meaning itself. Poetry promotes and engages these archetypal patterns—these potential forms in every person, that constellate meaning. We cannot know a poem without a grasp of the mythic energy that gathers in these primal and enduring patterns of consciousness. Such energy powers the patterns of universal import and myth's understanding remains also incomplete without the gnosis that poetry affords and insists on through these energy pockets.

The immediate or eventual pay-off of such a threshold crossing is that one risks being liberated from the spiral of delusions that can trap one for a lifetime and guarantee one's further suffering. However, a deeper level of awareness and enlightenment can liberate one, through poetry, from the veil of Maya that orchestrates all illusions. Poets and poetry may be understood in this vein of thought, as alchemists of the ensouled imagination. I may work the text, but I need to remember that at the same time the poem is working me, at times abrasively, yet helping me to uncover some crucial revelations of my and the world's deepest nature and mystery.

To sum up: **Poetry**

- Aids me in contemplating what is invisible but present in the world
- Invites me to bear witness
- Structures my past into a more coherent narrative by engaging both memory and history
- Aids me in reflecting more deeply on self and world
- Encourages me to look, to be aware of inner and outer realities simultaneously
- Offers me multiple visions: imaginal, perceptual, mythical, mimetic
- Creates a refuge for me in order to see more clearly and with a deeper sense of presence.

All, part or none of the above may be true for all; however, it carries a deep lived truth for me as well as a hope that it inspires you, the reader, to contemplate your own poetic self through the insights in both prose and poetry that populate this rich and diverse volume.

Endnote
[1] Pending publication, co-authored with Tim Donahue and Don Carlson.

Works Cited

Armstrong, Robert Plant. *Wellspring: On the Myth and Source of Culture.* Berkeley: U California P, 1975.

Campbell, Joseph. *Thou Art That: Transforming Religious Metaphor.* Ed. Eugene Kennedy. Novato, California: New World Library, 2001.

Lakoff, George. *Don't Think of an Elephant: Know Your Values and Frame the Debate.* Foreword by Howard Dean. White River Junction, Vermont: Chelsea Green Publishing, 2004.

Yeats, William Butler. "The Circus Animals' Desertion." *The Rag and Bone Shop of the Heart.* Eds. Robert Bly, James Hillman and Michael Meade. New York: HarperCollins, 1992. xxvii.

CHAPTER 20

MYTH AND WONDER

Recently I was reviewing some hand-written notes taken while rereading one of my favorite books, Josef Pieper's *Leisure: The Basis of Culture.* In it he speaks of leisure not as vacation or taking a break, but rather of establishing a temenos, a word that derives from temnein=to cut. In Latin, it is templem=a definite physical space cut off by enclosure or fencing. Plato's academy was one such temenos. The classroom of course is derived from such a beginning: an incubator, a place of conversation and perhaps, if things line up rightly, of conversion wherein a field of making and shaping is given a form and a presence. In the classroom ideas and images heat up, as in a kiln; they cross over, cross-reference and mingle in creative ways what we know with what we are still puzzled about. In my experience the classroom is a mythic space into which I have been entering both as student and as teacher since I was 5 years old. Sixty-five years have passed since that first threshold crossing; my life changed for the better with that first experience of learning formally.

But the classroom is also a place, I like to think, of wonder. When theologian Thomas Aquinas was writing a treatise on Aristotle, he came to the conclusion that "the philosopher is akin to the poet:

both are concerned with the mirandum—the 'wondrous,' the astonishing" (69), what arrests us, stops us in our tracks, and then, perhaps moves us to what we begin to love. But to enter this terrain one must step out from under "the canopy of work, for the practical moves of everyday and wonder do not mix well" (81); a suspension is needed. I suggest we must be willing to enter a mythic space so that things, ideas, images, passages from texts can step forward to make us wonder. The space of myth is the locale of surrender, of yielding to forces and presences beyond us and within us simultaneously. The space of myth is the habitation of narrative, history, revelation, dream, lunar rather than solar illumination and finally, renewal.

Now while myths are often prephilosophic, I think they share something profound with philosophy. Rather than ideas or concepts, myths are narratives that invite, encourage, even persuade us to wonder. Myths are wonder-ful narratives because they bring us to the edge of the familiar and push us over into wondering something new. In Plato's "Theatetus," Socrates has been introduced to a young bright man by his friend. Theatetus is the man's name and he is eager to learn. Socrates has been puzzling over the question: "What is knowledge?" and decides to take on the young man as his student and to work with him on this very difficult question.

Socrates sets the terms for the kind of learning he is interested in the two of them entering. He says to Theatetus, "…suppose we look at the question again in a quiet and leisurely spirit, not with any impatience but genuinely examining ourselves to see what we can make of these apparitions that present themselves to our minds" (860). Theatetus responds eagerly, even though he has been suffering to stay up with Socrates and add something of value to the session. When his teacher makes reference to several observations that puzzle the mind, Theatetus takes the opportunity to admit how he feels: "No, indeed, it is extraordinary how they set me wondering whatever they can mean. Sometimes I get quite dizzy with thinking of them" (860).

His response is music to the philosopher's ears, to which he responds by praising the friend who introduced the two of them: "That shows that Theodorus was not wrong in his estimate of your nature. This sense of wonder is the mark of the philosopher. Philosophy indeed has no other origin, and he was a good genealogist who made Iris the daughter of Thaumas" (860).

Leisure and wonder wed in this section of the dialogue; philosophy is born as the first and most important child of such a union. So let us push a bit further to see how myth is also a playmate in this family that Socrates has created as the origin of the impulse to learn.

Myths are formidable narratives with incredible shelf lives that express what an individual, in the case of a personal myth, or what a people, in a shared communal myth, wonder about themselves and themselves in relation to divinity, the dead, the natural order, ideas and the invisible but palpable qualities of experience.

So here is a story, almost a parable in fact, to help us out at this juncture: it has to do with animal perception, more specifically, with a crow searching out a juicy grasshopper to have for the day's main meal. Pieper introduces it in his reflections on leisure to help us understand something about learning and animal perception. I want to turn it a bit towards mythic consciousness, to which it also responds readily and holds up.

The grasshopper is no match for the speed, agility and force of the crow, but it has a very powerful defense against the crow or any other predator: stillness. The crow, we learn, cannot discern the grasshopper when the latter is not in motion, even when it is in plain view (83). Only when the grasshopper jumps does its form release itself from neighboring shapes; yet the crow does not even recognize the form of a resting grasshopper; it is only prepared to sense moving things. His range of sensibilities, or what I would also call "categories of awareness," is limited to motion, not to stasis. So, if the grasshopper keeps its wits about it and "plays dead," its resting form does not appear in the sense world of its predators. It cannot be found even if actively sought (83).

Now here is a leap into analogy: so it is with explaining personal myth. Let the myth assume the form of the grasshopper resting or lying in plain view; it is very much alive there but invisible in its stillness. Writing, if you will allow it to be a form of ritual, prods a part of the myth into the open, provokes it to jump for an instant. Now, in its motion we can see the moving form of the myth; it jumps into view for a brief moment, prodded by a rite of writing. This discursive activity, and I stress here cursive writing in long-hand rather than typing, animates or awakens the myth into action and finally, into meaning. And we snag just a part of this morsel in our beak;

seeing the grasshopper pulls us out of our familiar daily neighborhood of thought and perception. The grasshopper is certainly a source of nourishment for us, but it is also an occasion for allowing or inviting or instigating us to wonder. It is myth as metaphor; as metaphor it has the capacity to transport us to another arena of consciousness, of awareness, so that we see more by means of the grasshopper's instigation. Instigation leads to investigation, but not in analysis so much as in wonder. Leisure is the lynchpin that allows for such a disposition of consciousness to be open and receptive to the unknown.

So is this also true in the ritual act of reading, not for information but for transformation; we shift from "in" to "trans" and that makes all the difference. Let's say any book, but I am partial to conscripting a literary classic. The unopened poem is like the grasshopper in stillness; in this state the text cannot be seen by the reader, neither its content, but more importantly, its form. Only when in motion can the readerly crow in us begin to discern its presence; the poem enters one's sense world; in motion it gains presence—in an engaged conscious ritual of active reading. The text is the grasshopper you want to bring into view through the e-motion of reading. I have even heard readers say "this one passage jumped out and grabbed me." Such is the grasshopper when in motion; it jumps into your mythic view and stirs you to wonder. To talk *about* the text is only mildly satisfying. But to talk down, in and through it makes it hop, alive, across the page. The ritual of reading puts the poem in motion and motion makes it present. The poem is prodded into life by the rod of reading. And what it opens us to is a field of relations realigned in new ways that make us wonder. What I have attempted to describe is myth studies as field work of the most imaginative and engaging order. When one enters the field with reading field glasses on, there is no determining ahead of time what birds and beasts might come into view, to be wondered over.

This is where I am as teacher and learner 20 years into the Myth program.

Works Cited

Pieper, Josef. *Leisure: The Basis of Culture.* Trans. Gerald Malsbary. San Francisco: Ignatius P, 2009.

Plato. "The Theatetus." Trans. F.M. Cornford. In *Plato: The Collected Dialogues.* Ed. Edith Hamilton and Huntington Cairns. Bollingen Series LXXI. Princeton: Princeton UP, 1973. 845-919.

ABOUT THE AUTHOR

Dennis Patrick Slattery, Ph.D., has been teaching for 44 years, the last 20 in the Mythological Studies and Depth Psychology and Depth Psychotherapy programs at Pacifica Graduate Institute in Carpinteria, California. He is the author, co-author or co-editor of 23 books and hundreds of articles and book reviews in magazines, newspapers and collections of essays.

His books include: *The Idiot: Dostoevsky's Fantastic Prince; The Wounded Body: Remembering the Markings of Flesh; Grace in the Desert: Awakening to the Gifts of Monastic Life*. With Lionel Corbett he co-edited *Depth Psychology: Meditations in the Field* and *Psychology at the Threshold*. He co-edited with Glen Slater *Varieties of Mythic Experience: Essays on Religion, Psyche and Culture*; with Jennifer Leigh Selig he co-edited two volumes: *Reimagining Education: Essays on Reviving the Soul of Learning* and *The Soul Does Not Specialize: Revaluing the Humanities and the Polyvalent Imagination*. He has published five volumes of poetry: *Casting the Shadows: Selected Poems; Just Below the Water Line: Selected Poems*, both with accompanying CDs; *Twisted Sky: Selected Poems; The Beauty Between Words* co-authored with Chris Paris; and *Feathered Ladder: Selected Poems,* with Brian Landis. With Charles Asher he co-authored his first novel, *Simon's Crossing*. His two latest books include *Creases in Culture: Essays Toward a Poetics of Depth* and *Riting Myth, Mythic Writing: Plotting Your Personal Story*. His most recent book, *Our Daily Breach: Exploring Your Personal Myth Through Herman Melville's Moby-Dick*, is hunting for a publisher.

Dr. Slattery offers writing retreats on personal myth both in the United States and Europe through the work of Joseph Campbell and others. When not writing and teaching, Slattery and his sons ride their motorcycles across the back roads of the Texas Hill Country.

Contact: dslattery@pacifica.edu www.dennispslattery.com

ACKNOWLEDGMENTS

FORMAL ESSAYS

"Complex Nature and Mimetic Desire: Towards a Bio-Mimesis of Psyche and Matter." Conference sponsored by the Foundation for Mythological Studies: Nature and Human Nature: Changing Perspectives, March 16-18, 2007.

"Mythos, Logos, and the Politics of Justice." In a special issue of *Verbum Incarnatum* on *United States and Social Justice*. Volume 2, Number 1. San Antonio: University of Incarnate Word Publications, 2007. 50-59.

"Dante's Terza Rima in the *Divine Comedy:* The Road of Therapy," in *The International Journal of Transpersonal Studies*, vol. 27, Fall, 2008. 1-10.

"Mystic Faces, History's Traces: Joseph Campbell, Irish Mystic." *Spring Journal,* Winter 2008. 1-22.

"Violent Designs: Imagining Violence as Physical and Fictional." Mythology of Violence, Directed by Dr. Lori Pye. Pacifica Graduate Institute. Sponsored by the Foundation for Mythological Studies, April 4-6, 2008.

"Boxing Piety's Shadow." *Quadrant: Journal of the C.G. Jung Foundation for Analytical Psychology,* XXXVIX: 1 Winter, 2009. 53-62.

"Hestia: Goddess of the Heart(h)" To Pacifica Alumni Association, San Francisco, California, July 13, 2013.

"Myth, Method and Mythopoiesis: James Hillman's Archetypal

Psychology as Poetic Archeology." Celebration of the Work Of James Hillman Conference, The Dallas Institute of Humanities and Culture, Dallas, Texas. December 12, 2013.

"What is Myth and the God Image?" San Antonio Unitarian Universalist Church, San Antonio, Texas, July 20, 2014.

"Aesthetics, Politics, Ethics: An Emerging Trinity of Imagination in James Hillman's City and Soul. Celebration of the Work of James Hillman Conference. The Dallas Institute of Humanities and Culture, Dallas, Texas, October 16-18, 2014.

CULTURAL ESSAYS

"The Terrible Cost of Trust," delivered at Pacifica Graduate Institute's first Homecoming event, April 11, 2002 to 150 participants under the theme of "The World Behind the World."

"Holy Terror: The White Whale and the American Mythos." *Zion's Herald,* January/February 2006. 13.

"Lucy Under Glass: An Exhibit of the World's Most Complete Hominid". *Mythic Passages: The Magazine of the Imagination.* www.mhythicjourneys.org/newsletter_dec07_slattery.html

"Called to a Cohearant Life." Annual Saybrook University Jungian Studies Honorary Lecture. Houston Jung Center, Houston, Texas, November 7, 2014.

"The Myth of Memorial Day." Opinion, *Herald-Zeitung,* New Braunfels, Texas. Friday, May 30, 2014. 4.

"Growth: When a Myth No Longer Serves." Opinion, *Herald-Zeitung,* New Braunfels, Texas. Wednesday, August 20, 2014. 4.

"Poetry as Frame and as Form." Introduction to co-authored poetry volume: *Three Roads Taken: Selected Poems of Dennis Patrick Slattery, Timothy J. Donohue and Donald Carlson.* Forthcoming 2015.

"Myth and Wonder." Presented in a panel of Mythological Studies Faculty to participants of an Introduction Day, Pacifica Graduate Institute, August 29, 2014.